To Helen

A Traveller's Guide to Miracles in the Bible

IT'S A M

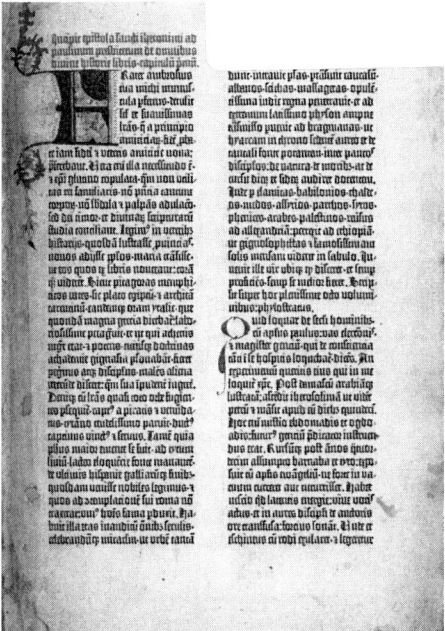

The Gutenberg Bible, 1455.[i]

John ×

John Murfitt

Austin Macauley Publishers®

LONDON • CAMBRIDGE • NEW YORK • SHARJAH

A CIP catalogue record for this title is available from the British Library.

ISBN 9781035888306 (Paperback)
ISBN 9781035888313 (ePub e-book)

www.austinmacauley.com

First Published 2025
Austin Macauley Publishers Ltd®
1 Canada Square
Canary Wharf
London
E14 5AA

Copyright Acknowledgements

For more information or if you have a comment about this book, please email the author: johnmurfitt@hotmail.com.

Cover photo: Sunrise over Funchal, Madeira. Photo kindly supplied by Jason Murfitt.
The apparent daily 'rising' of the sun is due to the rotation of the earth (Psalm 113:3).
It's a miracle.

About the Author

John Murfitt is enthusiastic about the subject of this book as with his others: *Two Destinies* (2022), *The Kingdom* (2023), and *Really?* (2023). After extensive research, each is a subject that he is burdened to share.

His past includes experience in the ministry, education, family life, and meeting the challenges all these have presented.

He lives near the south coast of Cornwall and in his retirement attends local churches, enjoys DIY, dog walking, writing, works with various village committees and keeps Pekin bantams. Occasionally, he plays golf, and he likes to travel.

He has been married to Ruth for more than 50 years and is proud of four sons and eight grandchildren.

When and where possible, he points others towards Christ.

Cornwall, 2025

This book is dedicated to Tim, Mark, Jason and Luke who have been and always will be special, and from whom I have learned so much.

Acknowledgements

I would like to sincerely thank those who have helped and encouraged me with this book.

I must especially thank Geoff, who is a brilliant Bible teacher and from whom I gain an immense amount, especially in terms of theology. As a respected critical friend, his Christian example and teaching causes me to examine very carefully the word of God, make adjustments to my text where necessary, and present my content in a truthful, clear and concise way. I am so thankful for all the time he gives me and the Lord in his life to study deeply and present truth clearly and in a way I and others can access.

In addition, I am grateful to staff at Austin Macauley for their support and direction to enable this book to be published. I would especially like to thank Phil for brilliant proofreading and for addressing editorial issues. I am grateful for the way he has challenged me.

Above all, I would like to thank my studious and ordained wife, Ruth, who has carefully checked this work, as with my previous books, and has always been an inspiration to me and a wonderful sounding board in all aspects of my script, more helpful and more challenging than she realises. She patiently supported my progress at every stage. She has made very useful suggestions in every chapter, for which I am very grateful.

I am also very grateful to Revd. Karl Carpani who has written a Foreword which is more favourable about me than I deserve. Karl is a brilliant artist, teacher and preacher with a tremendous knowledge of God's word. He walks by faith with his Lord and God. I worked and worshipped with him over a number of years and have greatly benefitted from his teaching and friendship.

Lastly, I would like to thank my four sons (to whom this book is dedicated), and unnamed people in this text whom I have encountered on my Christian journey and who have been a fitting example and inspiration to me. They have taught me so much; I trust I have been a good learner. Without them, I wouldn't be where I am, and this book would not have been written. Some have been especially patient with me over the years, keeping my feet on the ground and showing me by their lives and words the faithfulness of God, how to live as a Christian and how to love the word of God. I couldn't begin to apply theory to practice without them—and I am still learning much each day.

If any mistakes, weaknesses or inaccuracies have slipped into this book, I take full responsibility for them and I do apologise to you, the reader.

So, I am very blessed indeed, and I thank you, the reader, for taking on this book to consider its content and reach an informed decision about miracles. I can only imagine that you are as mystified as I am about some of them, but also trust you are as impressed as I am and in awe of our great God and of the grace he shows to this Earth and its people.

Table of Contents

Foreword   **15**

Textual Notes   *17*

Introduction   **19**

Early Days   **25**

1 Creation   *27*

2 Noah   *32*

Travelling Days   **41**

3 Moses Leaving Egypt and Crossing the Red Sea   *43*

4 Joshua, the Jordan and Jericho   *52*

Conflict Days   **59**

5 Gideon   *61*

6 David   *70*

Prophetic Days   **77**

7 Elijah   *79*

8 Jonah   *89*

Gospel Days   **95**

9 Jesus and the Widow of Nain's Son   *97*

10 Jesus and the Woman at the Well   *105*

Victory Days   **113**

11 Jesus and Palm Sunday   *115*

12 Jesus: The Crucifixion and the Resurrection   *123*

Outreach Days   **135**

    13 Peter and John   *137*

    14 Paul and Silas   *146*

Final Days   **153**

    15 The New Creation   *155*

Concluding Thoughts: Where Do We Go from Here?   **165**

Notes   **170**

Foreword

As a former parish priest of 17 years, a prison visitor, a former member of an international disaster response team, a police chaplain, and now a senior healthcare chaplain in London having just emerged from the Covid pandemic, I have witnessed life in the extremes, with hardship and suffering, loss and grief. At a time, when the cost of living is high, there is war, famine, climate crisis and disillusionment with leadership, many are praying earnestly and wholeheartedly for miracles.

I have known John Murfitt and his family for many years, first when I was a Curate in Biggin Hill, then as my Churchwarden in Green Street Green with his wife Ruth as my Associate Vicar. I have long known of John's attention to biblical truth and his passion for sharing his years of experience and wisdom as a former Headteacher and Free Church Minister.

John is a master craftsman in blending personal experience with scriptural truth and presenting these to an audience in an accessible and eloquent way.

John takes us on a journey that navigates biblical history and the significance of miracles in the lives of those who went before us. Through hardship and challenges not dissimilar to those felt by many of us today, we are transported back to these key historical events where God's intervention in human existence helps them navigate the twists, turns and challenges of seeking to live a life of obedience to God.

John summarises key biblical narratives and offers the reader final thoughts and questions on the significance of those interventions. He also highlights, how humanity benefits from their well-placed faith in a God who acts decisively and appropriately, with miraculous demonstrations of his grace and authority over creation and the created.

Revd Karl Carpani ✚

BA(Hons)ThM. Art History. CHCC,

Senior Chaplain Kings College Hospital NHS Foundation Trust, London.

Textual Notes

1. References are taken from the New International Version of the Bible, Anglicised, referred to as NIVUK, (The New International Version; Biblica, 1973, 1978, revised 1984 and 2011). For conciseness, the Old Testament and the New Testament are usually referred to as OT and NT.

2. References appear in the familiar format of book, chapter, verse (as in: John 3:16). If already referring to John chapter three, then reference to a verse will be indicated as, for example (v 16). A particular and popular version used is the KJV (King James Version), 1611. Other versions, where used, will be explained in the end notes.

3. Old Testament dating, where referred to, relies on John C. Whitcomb; Old Testament Kings and Prophets; BMH Books, 1977 and: bookshop.org/books/chart-old-testament-kings-and-prophets-paper; 2021. John C. Whitcomb (1924–2020) was a professor of theology and Old Testament at Grace Theological Seminary, Winona Lake, Indiana, USA, for 38 years.

4. On occasion, the full or concise Bible commentary of Matthew Henry (1662–1714), a theologian and nonconformist minister of a church in Chester, England is a very helpful sourcebook. The complete commentary was first published in 1706 in six volumes, entitled: *Exposition of the Old and New Testaments*.

   The edition I have mostly used is the one-volume concise edition published by Marshall, Morgan and Scott in 1980. Henry was competent in Latin and Greek from the age of nine. The full and concise editions are often referred to by my theologian sources.

5. If the reader follows up on my source references used in the end notes, please note a reduced reference World Wide Web address system is used such as *christianity.org*. The user's computer search engine should then automatically complete the web address as in:

https://www.christianity.org.uk/.

Introduction

I have always been keen to learn and if I can find answers to problems I encounter, then I am very happy indeed. At secondary school, I had some interesting experiences.

In physics, the teacher asked us all to stand around the walls of the science laboratory. Embarrassing as it was for 15-year-olds unless you were next to a girl you particularly liked, we were told to hold hands with the person to our left and right. The teacher joined in and said when he squeezed the hand of the person to his right, they were to pass on the squeeze and each one of us, when we felt the squeeze, was to pass it on round the circle.

With practice, we quickly carried this out and found we could get around the circle in a few seconds. Next, he said he would jump up and down and as the person on his right saw it and felt the movement, they were to do the same and keep jumping, and so on round the circle. This time, we had to pass the movement on, but then keep moving.

Very soon, we were all jumping up and down. The reason for these two experiments soon became clear. Our teacher said electricity is invisible but that is how it works. Atoms are activated and they affect their neighbour all the way from the power station to the appliance in the home, office, factory, or school.

In geography, the teacher asked us all to find a way to measure the wind speed or direction. Some in the class made a wind vane, others blew over a sheet of paper to show the principle of how moving air could lift an aeroplane wing. My friend and I decided on a more complex project: to make an anemometer.

Off we went to a scrap yard and for a small price we paid to extract from a crashed lorry its speedometer. At my home with the help of plastic cups, bamboo rods and copious amounts of balsa wood, glue and string; we got the device to work by giving the wind a little assistance by pushing the anemometer to get it going. The teacher was very pleased, as were we, with our efforts. We found that the effect of moving but invisible air could be seen.

In a film club, I ran after school one day a week, together with another friend—it was long before subscription TV, computers, the internet and social media—I encountered an interesting situation. It was a popular event. Each week I ordered a suitable film for hire, such as 'Deserts of the World,' 'How to Tie Knots' or 'How to Make Plastic Forks' or other subjects I now consider to be totally boringly pointless!

We were duly trained by a technician and then we operated quite a complex and very expensive 16 mm projector. How proud and important we felt! A powerful lamp shone through the film and frame by frame, the film progressed and things happened. I learned about threading the film, regulating the sound, and focussing the lens but what about light? Where, after it had illuminated a subject or the room, did it go?[2]

Some people think that it is impossible to believe what we can't see and that we can't believe what we can't prove, but what about my school experiences? Electricity and air are invisible, and the destination of light is impossible to determine, but we used them and made them work for us even though we didn't understand them!

When all has been discussed and reasoned, and learning has reached its limits, there are some things which cannot be fully understood or proven and must be accepted—by faith without scientific proof.

Miracles are like that.

By definition, a miracle is 'A surprising and welcome event that is not explicable by natural or scientific laws and is therefore considered to be the work of a divine agency.'[3]

A miracle is also explained as an 'Extraordinary and astonishing happening that is attributed to the presence and action of an ultimate or divine power.'[4]

The Bible includes history, poetry, and instructions for relationships, living and worship. It contains all that God wants us to know about him, ourselves, and salvation. There are some things that the Bible is: a book of love, justice, wisdom and common sense, and some things it isn't: a book of science or a book with answers to every problem.

Among other things, it teaches us about the establishment of the Kingdom of God[5] and has very precise teachings from Jesus about our choice of two destinies for the end of life.[6] It brings to the reader fear, faith and fact.

One remarkable fact about the Bible is that it contains miracles, and according to a 2011 poll, more than 90% of Christians believe miracles still take place.[7]

The list of contents for this book indicates in the chapter titles the Bible's unveiling of events, as the Bible, God's word, progresses from Genesis to Revelation. I have outlined eight periods of time and called them days in the way that we refer to periods of time in our lives. We may speak of the "days of my youth, days of plenty, exciting days or days of economic hardship".

In the last chapter considering Where do we go from here? we see the challenge of what we should do to change our thinking or to implement what we have learned from the selection of Bible miracles in this book.

The question to ponder is, 'How should our discoveries affect our lives?'

There are many miracles in the Bible, and I have selected just a few but they are representative of the types of miracles which we read of in the Scriptures. The contents page shows how there is a progression historically in the Bible from the beginning of all things to the end of life on Earth.

I have selected two examples from each of the time periods I have identified. Some are major events and have changed the world or the people in it, others are relatively minor events but are nonetheless included because they have something special to say to us.

C. S. Lewis has a very helpful contribution in relation to miracles in a Christian context:

'The fitness of the Christian miracles and their difference from mythological miracles lies in the fact that they show invasion by a power which is not alien. They are what might be expected to happen when she (*Nature*) is invaded not simply by a God, but by the God of Nature: by a power which is outside her jurisdiction not as a foreigner but as a sovereign. They proclaim that he who has come is not merely a king, but the King, her King and ours.'[8] (*Insertion and emphasis mine*)

It is this intervention by God into human affairs and our experience, we do well to keep at the back of our minds.

There is a service manual for almost everything technical that we buy. Everything from a car to a torch and from a central heating system to a watch. Often these manuals are very necessary and very helpful; at times they are complicated for the non-professional.

To the specialist, they may be easily understood, but to most people, they can become clear if given time, thought and careful study. I regard the Bible as being like that. It takes time and effort to understand it, but it is the instruction manual for life. It is authoritative and utterly reliable and infallible, because of the input of the Holy Spirit who has prompted and watched over the writers as they wrote.

God knew the importance of the outcome, so it had to be correct and easy to understand with the Holy Spirit's help; by all people of all ages and cultures for all of time. One example of this correctness from Scripture is given in a letter from Paul who writes as a senior Apostle teaching his friend, the young pastor, Timothy.

'All Scripture is God-breathed and is useful for teaching, rebuking, correcting and training in righteousness.' (2 Timothy 3:16)

There are no areas of the world, nor, indeed, of this country, where miracles are likely to occur. Neither are there times in the past, present or future when they occurred or are likely to occur.

I am encouraged to read a recently published book by Jill Duff, the Anglican Bishop of Lancaster in the diocese of Blackburn; in answer to a question posed to her about the possibility of people believing in miracles, whilst she was visiting the West Country:

'We're in Cornwall, the land of the saints. People come to Cornwall because it's a place of miracles, a thin place where heaven seems close to earth.'[9]

In this book, miracles in the Bible will be considered individually to see why God chose on occasion to work differently from the original laws he established. Therefore, we must investigate the Bible and God's ways of working with confidence and with an open mind.

As with all Scripture, we must make up our own minds, but bear in mind the views of others, and avoid two extremes. These are to believe everything by blind faith without requiring any understanding and explanation, and disbelieving everything and confining it to the realms of fantasy.

The Bible is a book revealing God and his will for people on the earth but it requires faith to believe it.

Paul also said to Timothy:

'Do your best to present yourself to God as one approved, a worker who does need to be ashamed and who correctly handles the word of truth.' (2 Timothy 2:15)

I trust we do the same.

Questions to consider:

1. What is a miracle?
2. Do we believe in miracles?
3. If Scripture is God-breathed, does this mean it is without mistakes?

Early Days

1 Creation

'In the beginning God—' (Genesis 1:1)
Full Story: (Genesis 1, 2:1–7)

In The Sound of Music,[10] Julie Andrews begins,
'Let's start at the very beginning,
A very good place to start.'

I am, therefore, doing the same in this study of miracles. I am looking at creation—the start of everything. This is the beginning of the world which has, regarding people, two starts: the creation of the first people where sin leads to the Fall and estrangement from God, and the second start which takes place after the flood in which we see those who survive begin life on Earth again.

I wonder if God was sad and disappointed in his creation of people because, at the end of the age, this first creation with its two starts is replaced, redeemed and renewed by the new creation. The Fall affected not only people but the physical world which also changed. So, we read in the NT of a new heaven and a new earth.

I have, therefore, referred to the *Creation* parts (i) and (ii). This is part (i). In chapter 15, there is the New Creation: part (ii).

Before a committee is active, it establishes its Terms of Reference and I must do the same. Creation is described as having two meanings in the Oxford Languages Dictionary:

(1) 'The action or process of bringing something into existence.' The example of the word in use is: *Creation* of a coalition government.

(2) 'The creating of the universe, especially when regarded as an act of God. The example of the word in use here is: the big bang was the moment of the *Creation*, and therefore the work of God.'[11]
I think this second example is fascinating and included to please a

particular scientific view. However, it does name God as being behind creation, and creation as the start of life.

Creation is a story in the spiritual books of the major religions[12] but is introduced and accurately described by the Bible in Genesis. This is the account which is inspired by God and carries true authority from God, endorsed by Jesus in a resurrection appearance on the Emmaus Road, in which the first book of Moses is Genesis.

'And beginning with Moses and all the Prophets, he explained to them what was said in all the Scriptures concerning himself.' (Luke 24:27)

Creation is God's first Bible miracle affecting people. We are not given a date for the beginning, but we are told that when it was, God was there.

The first four words of the Bible, **'In the beginning, God—'** (Genesis 1:1), therefore, set the scene for all that is to follow. The Bible is a collection of books which give us all that we need to know for salvation. It meets the needs of people even if it doesn't meet everyone's wants in terms of detailed information explaining how God achieved the Creation.

In terms of the world and the universe, the Bible does reveal God at work, after he had created heaven as his home, and populated it with the angelic order. God, then created the world for his pleasure and people to love him and worship him on Earth as his own family.

The creation of the heavens, including the creation of the earth, exhibits the wonder and glory of God as the Psalms proclaim:

'LORD, our LORD…You have set your glory in the heavens.' (Psalms 8:1)

'The heavens declare the glory of God; the skies proclaim the work of his hands.' (Psalms 19:1)

'The heavens proclaim his righteousness, for he is a God of justice.' (Psalms 50:6)

'The heavens praise your wonders, LORD, your faithfulness too.' (Psalms 89:5)

The Bible lists the six days of creation before he rested on the seventh.

'For in six days, the LORD made the heavens and the earth, the sea, and all that is in them, but he rested on the seventh day. Therefore, the LORD blessed the Sabbath day and made it holy.' (Exodus 20:11)

The logical order of God's creation of the Earth is given, including the creation of light and darkness, water and sky, land and vegetation, sun, moon and stars, water creatures and flying creatures, land creatures and wild creatures, and last of all people. To be precise, two people.

In all of his creation, it is only of these two: Adam and Eve whom God said were, in terms of their image, like himself. 'So, God created mankind in his own image, in the image of God he created them; male and female he created them.'

(Genesis 1:27) In doing so, God made people so they could reflect God in their personality and characteristics. They had feelings and could make choices.

Creation was perfect and everything was in harmony, exactly as God wanted it to be so having created it in its various stages, he pronounced at each stage that it was good. God makes it clear he created everything for his glory.

In fact, 'The whole earth is full of his glory.' (Isaiah 6:3 c)

In being given free will, people could choose to obey God, and this was his intention. Despite its beauty and complexity, creation happened very simply and would continue securely (Genesis 8:22).

God commanded and life came into being. 'By the word of the LORD the heavens were made, their starry host by the breath of his mouth.' (Psalm 33:6)

To put it another way, God 'calls into being things that were not' (Romans 4:17c), and as we consider this great act of God, 'By faith we understand that the universe was formed at God's command so that what is seen was not made out of what was visible.' (Hebrews 11:3)

The Bible is full of references to God's action in creation and informs us he is fully deserving of our wonder and praise, 'You are worthy, our LORD and God, to receive glory and honour and power, for you created all things, and by your will, they were created and have their being.' (Revelation 4:11)

Creation, as recorded in Genesis chapter one, centres around God the Father who brought things into being by just speaking the word, but he was not alone. As the choice of the plural word us makes clear, Jesus his Son and the Holy Spirit were with him.

God said, 'Let us make mankind in our image, in our likeness so that they may rule over the fish…the birds…the livestock…the wild animals and…all the creatures that move along the ground' (Genesis 1:26), 'And the Spirit of God was hovering over the waters.' (Genesis 1:2 b) (*Emphasis mine*).

Creation and the start of life were progressing very well. God had a purpose and achieved his purpose. Not only was mankind the pinnacle of God's creation and given the *dominion* (KJV) or *rule* (NIVUK). But we also read of the task assigned, 'The LORD God took the man and put him in the Garden of Eden to work it and take care of it' ('work it and keep it' ESV).[13] (Genesis 2:15)

I have relatives who are wonderful cooks. One, who comes to mind, has an unflappable nature and is able to make something out of very little resources: essentially and colloquially, *out of nothing*. This is the gift of Christian hospitality and catering skills in action, and the outcome is a delicious meal. I know from experience!

In the same way, but on an incomparable scale, it was easy for the Trinity: Father, Son and Holy Spirit to achieve Creation out of nothing, as told in the first chapter of Genesis. All it took was to say the word and amazing things came into being. This was a truly magnificent, complex and awesome miracle. Undoubtedly, as I consider creation, it will "take my breath away!"[14]

Final thoughts

In this study based on Genesis, there are several key things to note on the subject of creation, which are both wonderful in scope and intricate in detail:

[1] As the first words of the Bible tell us, God has always existed (Genesis 1:1).

[2] God made everything, and mankind is the pinnacle of his creation (Genesis 1:27).

[3] Because he is omnipotent, and he is God, all it took to create was a word from him for things to come into being (Genesis 1:3, v6, v9, v11, v14, v20, v24 and 2:6). 'For he spoke, and it came to be, he commanded and it stood firm' (Psalms 33:9).

Trying to understand Creation may stretch us intellectually, and it may stretch us spiritually, but this is where faith is needed. As the father of a boy with a disability said to Jesus, 'I do believe; help me overcome my unbelief!' (Mark 9:24b).

It is a mark of our maturity and of our desire to seek God and wisdom, to say we understand a little and to acknowledge that we need God to help us understand more.

Questions to consider:

1. If we were in a Bible study with Jesus, what do you think would happen?
2. Do we think the six days of Creation in Genesis are six days of 24 hours?
3. Do we think Creation was made by God speaking or do we think he used actions and matter?

Noah found favour in the eyes of the LORD (Genesis 6:8).
Full Story: (Genesis 6–8)

I live in the beautiful county of Cornwall, England, and many of the visitors pay to see the splendid gardens in this county which are attractive and open to the public right around the year. Even in the winter season, when many plants and trees are resting, the gardens hold a fascination as if they are waiting for the temperature to lift and then burst forth with their own unique splendour.

One of these is Heligan Gardens. This is a reclamation project returning long-term a "lost garden" to Victorian grandeur covering a vast area of 200 acres near Mevagissey on the South Coast. At any time of year, it seems to be kept beautifully and in perfect shape.

The whole world began in perfect shape. There was a beautiful garden in a beautiful world and two beautiful and perfect people in it. Everything brought pleasure to their Creator. There was harmony and peace. The human beings were granted free will but with a condition attached to one named thing they must not do.

As created life in Genesis unfolds, Adam was told he must not eat the fruit from one of the two trees God planted in the centre of the Garden of Eden, 'The tree of the knowledge of good and evil.' (Genesis 2:9b).

The other tree, the tree of life held no such prohibition. Adam was designed to live forever, but if he ate fruit from the forbidden tree God told him it would lead to his death.

As time progressed, the newly created creatures were brought to Adam for him to name and select one as his helper (v20). When he didn't find a helper amongst them, God anesthetised Adam and

'Took one of the man's ribs and then closed up the place with flesh. Then the LORD God made a woman from the rib—' (v21b, v22a)

Eve was, therefore, created from 'Out of the man' (v23c).

In this first male and female relationship, as the pattern for people to come, there was oneness and no self-consciousness (v24–25). God's principles of free will and freedom with responsibility are established, but the next development in the story records a serious break in their relationship with God.

Satan comes onto the scene and tempts Adam and Eve to defy God and to want to be like God, as he himself had done (Isaiah 14:12, Ezekiel 28:15–18 and Revelation 12:7–9). His pride led to his downfall, and it led to that of Adam and Eve, 'In his pride the wicked man does not seek him; in all his thoughts there is no room for God' (Psalms 10:4).

Pride is sin; sin leads to the Fall; and this is inherited by all mankind and causes creation to change 'Cursed is the ground because of you; through painful toil, you will eat food from it all the days of your life. It will produce thorns and thistles for you—' (Genesis 3:17b, v18a).

It became imperfect and would remain so until the end of the age, and though creation began perfect, as Ken Ham (b. 1951), Australian Creationist and President of Answers in Genesis, writes, 'The situation did not remain perfect because the first man, Adam, rebelled against the Creator, resulting in all of creation suffering from the effects of sin and the curse.'[15]

The Fall affects all people, as the Apostle Paul wrote:

'All have sinned and fall short of the glory of God' (Romans 3:23).

The Fall also affects the created world:

'For the creation was subjected to frustration, not by its own choice, but by the will of the one who subjected it…We know that the whole creation has been groaning as in the pains of childbirth right up to the present time' (Romans 8:20, v22).

Jesus told the Pharisees in a heated debate with them, 'You belong to your father, the devil, and you want to carry out your father's desires' (John 8:44).

Paul told the Christians in Ephesus that we will all have struggles in our Christian lives with 'Powers of this dark world and (*we are opposed by*) the spiritual forces of evil' (Ephesians 6:12b) (*Insertion and emphasis mine*). He warns Christians in Corinth to be very watchful because, 'Satan himself masquerades as an angel of light' (2 Corinthians 11:14). He plans always to deceive.

This was not the peace and calm experienced by the first people in the first-created garden setting. Once the Fall had happened, life on Earth became very different. People multiplied but the harmony of a close friendship with God had stopped. Sin, suffering, death and imperfection in the whole of creation had entered the world and became the inheritance of all its population for all time.

This is the background to the story of Noah. We find that people as sinners do not seek God or his will for their lives but rather they do what they want to do and ignore God and certainly don't want him to tell them what to do. But there was one person in all this wickedness who would not go along with the ways that people around him were choosing to live.

That was Noah. Whilst we read, 'The LORD saw how great the wickedness of the human race had become on the earth, and that every inclination of the thoughts of the human heart was only evil all the time' (Genesis 6:5).

He was also saying he was going to deal with it, 'I will wipe from the face of the earth the human race I have created—and with them the animals, the birds and the creatures that move along the ground—for I regret that I have made them' (v7). In contrast, there was the character of Noah. 'Noah found favour in the eyes of the LORD' (v8).

Noah was righteous and lived in harmony with God and listened to God but people around him were 'Corrupt in God's sight and...full of violence' (v11).

God sees what happens on earth and when he is ready, he acts. I know as a teacher that this is how I am. When I was teaching, I only accepted classroom noise for so long until it reached a certain level, which showed me not much work was being done. Then, I took action to quieten things down.

God watched, waited, then intervened and told Noah to take action: to build an ark (v14). It was to keep him and his wife and family safe and to ensure that they and creatures in the air and on land, had a new start.

God gave Noah the plans with precise measurements from which to build, and he was commanded to take into the ark two of every creature, male and female, and food for them and his family for a long period, suggested by the words, 'Store it away—' (v21).

It seems that God would be very active in the gathering of creatures and cause them to come to Noah; so his job upon completion of the ark was to accept them in and settle them into enclosures he had prepared for them, 'Two of every kind of bird, of every kind of animal and of every kind of creature that moves along the ground will come to you to be kept alive' (v20).

The Christian resource group, Ark Encounter, informs that 'Nowhere does it say that Noah built the ark by himself. He may have hired a crew of craftsmen who used both metal and wooden tools, which the Bible records they had available' (Genesis 4:22).

Noah did all that God asked him to do (Genesis 6:22 and 7:5), and preached righteousness to those watching him (2 Peter 2:5), as he steadily built the ark.

Another interesting fact is that the ark may well have been built on dry ground since there is no mention of building it where it could be launched into water. It also seems that people had not experienced rain or floods prior to this event.

The book of Hebrews tells us, 'By faith, Noah, when warned about *things not yet seen*, in holy fear built an ark to save his family' (Hebrews 11:7) (*Emphasis mine*).

Another Christian resource group, Got Questions suggests:

'Rain could be the correct understanding of "things not yet seen", or it could be referring to the flood in general.'[16]

Genesis 7 gives us an order of events as the story unfolds.

Noah went into the ark with all the animals, and God told him that after seven days he would 'Send rain on the earth for forty days and forty nights' (v4).

Noah and his family were to enter the ark, 'To escape the waters of the flood' (v7b).

'And after the seven days the floodwaters came on the earth' (v10).

'The springs of the great deep burst forth, and the floodgates of heaven were opened' (v11b).

'For 40 days, the flood kept coming and…lifted the ark high above the earth…and the ark floated on the surface of the water' (v17–18).

'All the high mountains under the entire heavens were covered' (v19).

'Every living thing on the face of the earth was wiped out; people and animals and the creatures that move along the ground and the birds in the air. Only Noah was left, and those with him in the ark' (v23).

'The waters flooded the earth for a hundred and fifty days' (v24).

Genesis 8 continues the story.

'But God remembered Noah…and the waters receded. Now, the springs of the deep and the floodgates of the heavens had been closed, and the rain had stopped falling from the sky' (v1–2).

'Then, Noah knew that the water had receded from the earth' (v11b).

God said to Noah, 'Come out of the ark, you and your wife and your sons and their wives. Bring out every kind of living creature that is with you…so they can multiply on the earth and be fruitful and increase in number on it' (v15–17).

The LORD said, 'Never again will I destroy all living creatures, as I have done' (v21b).

Noah worships God who makes an amazing promise, 'As long as the earth endures, seedtime and harvest, cold and heat, summer and winter, day and night will never cease' (v22).

There is no wonder Thomas O. Chisholm (1866–1960) writes in the famous hymn 'Great is Thy faithfulness' verse two:

'Summer and winter and springtime and harvest

Sun, moon and stars in their courses above

Join with all nature in manifold witness To Thy great faithfulness, mercy and love.'[17]

This amazing miracle of Noah and the ark, which led to the family and animals being safe and able to make a new start to life on the Earth unfolds before us, but we must note two more things.

Firstly, it is a major miracle but contains in its detail a collection of lesser miracles.

Secondly, it is endorsed in NT days by Jesus and Peter as being authentic;[18] (It is always a good principle to see if and where the NT comments on the OT!) This silences the argument that Creation, or other OT accounts, was a myth since we cannot charge Jesus with telling anything but the truth. He speaks of it as a real event and points out that the world will be just as Godless and God-avoiding in the days preceding his Second Coming.

He said, 'For in the days before the flood, people were eating and drinking, marrying and giving in marriage, up to the day Noah entered the ark; and they knew nothing about what would happen until the flood came and took them all away. That is how it will be at the coming of the Son of Man' (Matthew 24:38–39).

The raven and dove, and the appearance of the rainbow are also all woven into Genesis to help complete the picture. The whole account of Noah and the ark-building is a miracle, and God was behind all the miraculous parts of this event but there are some further particular details which make the whole story even more special. These are worthy of attention.

Final thoughts

[1] Noah's life and faith, as Genesis records, was righteous and blameless (Genesis 6:9, v18 and 7:1), and appears to cover his family as well as himself (Genesis 6:10, v18, 7:1 and 8:18).

[2] Noah started a family at 500 years old (Genesis 5:32), and they presumably helped him to build the ark. He was 600 (Genesis 7:6) when the flood came. The best calculation for the date of the flood is 2304 BC.[19]

[3] It is likely no one had ever built a boat of this size before, certainly not inland and big enough to house two of each of the world's numerous variety of creatures (Genesis 6:14).

[4] There was a canopy of water overhead, springs rising and rain descending (Genesis 7:11–12). No rain had been seen before these 40 days of rain (v4).

[5] There was one window (Genesis 8:6), and one door in the ark, and when the animals and people were safely in, God was the one who shut the door (Genesis 7:16).

[6] The flood was seven metres higher than the top of the mountains (v20).

[7] God sent a special wind to stop the waters rising beyond a certain point (Genesis 8:1).

[8] The untamed dove lets Noah handle it (v9).

[9] All the creatures got on well together in the months in the ark (v17) and supplies didn't run out (Genesis 6:21 and 8:19).

[10] After exiting the ark, God saw and smelled Noah's incense and worship and resolved never to flood the whole earth again and never to wipe out the Earth's population again (Genesis 8:21). This was God's promise and as a sign and seal to this promise, he created a rainbow for the first time (Genesis 9:13).

God keeps his promises. 'Not one of all the LORD's good promises to Israel failed; was fulfilled' (NIVUK); 'All came to pass' (KJV) (Joshua 21:45).

Questions to consider:

1. Who first sinned, the serpent, Eve or Adam?
2. Was the flood: because of sin, a natural disaster, or a fable (Genesis 6, especially, v1–8)?
3. Was the flood localised to Israel or worldwide?

Travelling Days

3 Moses Leaving Egypt and Crossing the Red Sea

'God led the people—' (Exodus 13:18a)
Full Story: (Exodus 10–14)

Over a number of years of driving, in pre-SatNav days, I found that it was hard to follow a map and drive safely at the same time, so my wife was my navigator using a detailed map of the UK. I have to be honest and say there were sometimes heated words between us and sometimes I failed to follow her instructions for a variety of reasons.

Then came the days of the *SatNav*, and if programmed correctly a professional voice which never got flustered and never chided or praised was now my navigator. This usually worked out well but not always, again for a variety of reasons.

When errors in not following instructions occurred, the voice would say, 'Turn around when possible.'

This happened and we got back on course.

As we move into our second chapter, we find that in his wisdom and mercy, God gave people a second start on the earth. Adam and Eve had the first start but failed to honour God and the second start when Noah came out of the ark, began well, but soon led to people pleasing themselves and not obeying God as their LORD. We read in Genesis of patriarchs such as Abraham,[20] Isaac, and Jacob.

The next was one of Jacob's sons, Joseph. His brothers, in their jealousy and anger towards Joseph, had sold him as a slave to nomadic traders, but thankfully, he was sold again to a respectable and influential family in Egypt. As the account unfolded, he found that he was in the right place at the right time to ensure his family was safe and protected in this foreign land.

He arranged for his family and servants of Jacob, his father, to move from the Promised Land of Canaan to Egypt to survive a life-threatening famine.

Rising to the position of the equivalent of Prime Minister, Joseph said to his humbled brothers, 'You intended to harm me, but God intended it for good to accomplish what is now being done, the saving of many lives' (Genesis 50:20).

The king, Pharaoh, was very considerate to the Israelites because of Joseph and treated them well.

All of this unfolds towards the end of Genesis, and continues into Exodus, without named leaders of the Israelites, but then, Moses comes into the picture. In summary, Chapters 1–18 narrate the history of Egyptian bondage, the Exodus from Egypt, and the journey to Mount Sinai under the leadership of Moses.[21]

The Israelites retained their own identity and prospered in Goshen, a fertile part of Egypt, for a number of generations; but under a different Pharaoh who was not concerned about how the Israelites came to be in his kingdom, made them slaves to the Egyptians, who found them too numerous to control, and the Egyptians, and especially their Pharaoh, felt threatened by their increasing numbers (Exodus 1:11).

Moses was brought up in the royal palace (Exodus 2:10) but in his heart he was still an Israelite or Hebrew, but was quite hot-tempered. One day when he saw an Egyptian mistreating a fellow Hebrew, he killed the Egyptian and tried to hide the murder, but then he was discovered and had to flee into the desert where he became established in a new life as a shepherd (v15).

It was the C 13th BC,[22] and the Israelites who were cruelly treated to hard manual brickmaking labour, could stand the servitude no more. 'The Israelites groaned in their slavery and cried out, and their cry for help because of their slavery went up to God. God heard their groaning and he remembered his covenant with

Abraham, with Isaac and with Jacob. So, God looked on the Israelites and was concerned about them' (Exodus 2:23–25).

This shepherding in the wilderness proved to be all part of the preparation of Moses used by God for him to become a shepherd of people: the leader of the Israelites. One day an angel, synonymous with God, appeared to him in a burning bush. This miraculously burned without being destroyed, and the angel told him he had been chosen by God to lead his people back to the Promised Land. Moses was reluctant to take on the role, but God had a conversation with Moses from the bush and promised to support him in the task (Exodus 3:10–12).

Then, after requesting and receiving from God miraculous signs to prove his words could be believed, Moses trusted that God was with him and returned from the desert of Midian to Egypt.

We read, 'So, Moses took his wife and sons, put them on a donkey and started back to Egypt. And he took the staff of God in his hand' (Exodus 4:20).

God knew Pharaoh would not easily submit to allowing the Israelites to leave Egypt because they were too useful for brickmaking for the new cities being created by Pharaoh.

God gave Moses a promise that he would enable them to leave Egypt, and this probably kept Moses going forward and said, 'I know that the king of Egypt will not let you go unless a mighty hand compels him. So, I will stretch out my hand and strike the Egyptians with all the wonders that I will perform among them. After that, he will let you go' (Exodus 3:19–20).

Because Pharaoh refused to set the Israelites free, God punished him, sending 10 plagues to destroy Egypt. Nine plagues, all miracles in themselves, failed to persuade Pharaoh as he made and broke promises to let the people go. The 10th and last plague was the most devastating and was the one which changed Pharaoh's mind.

As we see in the media, dictators and empires rise and, eventually, they fall. Rarely is there a godly, or even a good-living, dictator working for the good of others, and especially not one who will acknowledge God as LORD. And so it was with Pharaoh, king of Egypt. He was heartless and refused to let the people go until so many Egyptians died in the 10th plague: the death of selected people and livestock. This struck at the heart of Pharaoh as he was personally affected.

When night came, God sent the angel of death to kill the firstborn sons of the Egyptians. God told Moses, together with his brother Aaron who spoke for Moses, to order the Israelite families to sacrifice a lamb and smear the blood on the doorframes of their houses. In this way, the angel would see the blood and know to pass over the homes of the Israelites.[23] Even Pharaoh and his queen lost their eldest son (Exodus 12:29).

During the night, Pharaoh reached his limit of endurance and sent for Moses and Aaron and told them the Israelites were free to leave. They had been in Egypt for 430 years and now numbered 600,000 men plus women and children. They also had great numbers of livestock.[24] The Egyptians then gave them vast quantities of silver, gold and clothing (v35), to hasten the Israelite's departure.

So, they left with the food they had prepared in advance for the journey which they anticipated would happen. The British Library's 'Escape from Egypt,' tells us:

'Moses had reminded his people that they had to leave in a hurry and that their bread dough would not have time to rise. They were therefore told to make unleavened bread (bread made without yeast). To commemorate this, unleavened bread is still eaten by Jewish people during the annual Passover festival.'[25]

Goshen to the crossing point of the Red Sea was about 250 miles (400 Km) according to Steven Rudd, Canadian Christian Minister, Evangelist and Biblical archaeologist.[26] God was the one leading the vast number of people and to protect his people he didn't lead them by the shortest route which went through hostile Philistine territory. He knew that might lead to war, causing them to want to return to Egypt. Here we meet our keywords for this miracle, **'God led the people—'** (Exodus 13:18a).

He led them around the desert and towards the Red Sea, sometimes called the Sea of Reeds. Rudd suggests this would have taken 25 days of travel from Goshen.[27]

As the people journeyed, and he thought about his loss of free labourers, Pharaoh regretted letting the Israelites go. He called his army and set off to capture and return the Israelites by his chariot-led army complete with horsemen and foot soldiers, and bring them back into slavery in Egypt. They caught up with the Israelites at Pi Hahiroth (Exodus 14:10) bordering the Red Sea.

Here the Israelites realised they had a challenging situation with the sea in front of them and the Egyptian army behind them. They despaired with nowhere to go, so God provided an impenetrable cloud to separate the army from the Israelites, as a temporary measure to keep his people safe. Their outlook was desperate; a miracle was needed!

The people complained to God and to Moses and said they wished they had stayed in Egypt, where they didn't have this crisis and had plenty of food (Numbers 11:5), so Moses spoke firmly and:

'Answered the people, "Do not be afraid. Stand firm and you will see the deliverance the LORD will bring you today. The Egyptians you see today you will never see again. The LORD will fight for you; you need only to be still". Then the LORD said to Moses, "Why are you crying out to me? Tell the Israelites to move on. Raise your staff and stretch out your hand over the sea to divide the water so that the Israelites can go through the sea on dry ground. I will harden the hearts of the Egyptians so that they will go in after them. And I will gain glory through Pharaoh and all his army, through his chariots and his horsemen. The Egyptians will know that I am the LORD when I gain glory through Pharaoh, his chariots and his horsemen'" (Exodus 14:13–18).

Facing the Red Sea God said to Moses, 'Raise your staff and stretch out your hand over the sea to divide the water so that the Israelites can go through the sea on dry ground' (v16).

We see here the staff brought from his shepherding in the wilderness (Exodus 4:20), is now used on the banks of the sea. Moses did as he was commanded (Exodus 14:21), he raised his hand and God worked all night and drove back the sea, Pharaoh and his army followed in their ignorance and arrogance and charged after the Israelites. Once they were all in the middle of the sea on the dry land, God threw them into confusion. He jammed the wheels of their chariots so that they had difficulty driving. They knew that something was seriously working against them. And the Egyptians said, "Let us get away from the Israelites! The LORD is fighting for them against Egypt" (24b, v25).

Moses raised his hand and staff again, and the sea 'went back to its place' (v27), swallowing up and destroying Pharaoh and his entire army. The story of the escape from Egypt is commemorated by Jewish people every year during the festival of Passover. In this way, the idea of freedom and God's deliverance is kept alive and is continually passed on in family meals by adults to their children.[28]

Salem Web Networks tells us, 'When the Israelites see the power of God they put their faith in God and in Moses and sing a song of praise to the LORD for the crossing of the sea'[29] (v31, 15:1–18).

We must note miraculous elements to this amazing story of God leading the people up to and through the Red Sea.

Final thoughts

[1] God took the initiative to come from heaven to Earth, 'So I have come down to rescue (*the Israelites)* from the hand of the Egyptians and to bring them up out of that land into a good and spacious land' (Exodus 3:8a) (*Insertion mine*). The French artist, James Tissot (1836–1902), paints a famous and challenging picture of the Red Sea crossing which he calls, *The Waters are Divided.*[30]

[2] Instead of taking a short route to the sea, God took his people a long route to avoid a war in a dangerous Philistine country (Exodus 13:17–18). Another famous painting by Nicholas Poussin (1594–1665), in the French Baroque style called *The Crossing of the Red Sea*, adds, 'God sometimes brings us the long way because we are mentally, emotionally, and spiritually unprepared to face what awaits us along the short route or at the end of our journey.'[31]

[3] God hardened Pharaoh's heart until he learned that God, the God of the Israelites, is the LORD (Exodus 14:4). He lost his life in learning this lesson.

[4] God wanted to establish the Passover through the final plague (Exodus 12:11), not only for it to be remembered by the Israelites,[32] as part of the Old Covenant, but also as an annual event. At the time of Christ on earth, God planned it so that Jesus would die on this festival weekend to establish the New Covenant (Hebrews 9:15).

[5] God wanted to show the people they had to learn to trust him, and there was no turning back, not even for the food they remembered:

'We remember the fish we ate in Egypt at no cost—also the cucumbers, melons, leeks, onions and garlic' (Numbers 11:5).

[6] God wanted the people to learn they could trust him to lead them and despite the intransigent Pharaoh and then the impassable Red Sea, he would deliver them to the Promised Land. God said, 'I will stretch out my hand and strike the Egyptians with all the

wonders that I will perform among them. After that, he will let you go' (Exodus 3:20).

[7] The cloud was amazing. 'By day the LORD went ahead of them in a pillar of cloud to guide them on their way and by night in a pillar of fire to give them light so that they could travel by day or night. Neither the pillar of cloud by day nor the pillar of fire by night left its place in front of the people' (Exodus 13:21–22).

As the Egyptians almost caught up with the Israelites at Pi Hahiroth near the sea, the cloud[33] moved from in front of the people to a position behind them. 'Throughout the night the cloud brought darkness to the one side and light to the other side. So, neither went near the other all night long' (Exodus 14:20).

God, then, and always, wants people to be led by him and say, 'Come…let us walk in the light of the LORD' (Isaiah 2:5).

[8] The water was amazing. The water standing up as a wall was another obvious miracle. 'Then, Moses stretched out his hand over the sea, and all that night the LORD drove the sea back with a strong east wind and turned it into dry land. The waters were divided, and the Israelites went through the sea on dry ground, with a wall of water on their right and on their left' (Exodus 14:29).

[9] 2.5 million people (600,000 men), and thousands of animals crossed over the sea and got safely to the other side and they were followed by Pharaoh and his vast army who were on the dry seabed when the waters returned (v26–29).

The Israelites were completely safe and the Egyptians were completely destroyed. It can be hard to understand why some people had to die, but further on in Exodus, God states his sovereignty. 'I will have mercy on whom I will have mercy, and I will have compassion on whom I will have compassion' (Exodus 33:19).

[10] The Passover and crossing of the Red Sea have always been central in Jewish history. At times, God and his prophets reminded the people of these important events, 'Then, his people

recalled the days of old, the days of Moses and his people—where is he who brought them through the sea,' and we note that they did not stumble (Isaiah 63:11, v13b).

Paul writing to the Christians at Corinth said, 'For I do not want you to be ignorant of the fact, brothers and sisters, that our ancestors were all under the cloud and that they all passed through the sea' (1 Corinthians 10:2).

Despite this amazing miracle which pointed them in faith to Christ (v4), God was not pleased with most of them because they didn't live by or continue in faith and so God prevented them from entering the Promised Land.

To live a life pleasing to God and to have faith is a challenge to us all!

Questions to consider:

1. Was Joseph right to conceal his identity from his brothers?
2. Do we think the waters stood vertically at the sides of Moses' path across the Red Sea?
3. Was it right to allow Pharaoh and his army to die in the sea?

4 Joshua, the Jordan and Jericho

'Do not say a word until the day I tell you to shout. Then, shout!' (Joshua 6:10b)

Full story: (Joshua 5:1, v13–15 and 6:1–20)

In my teaching career, I encountered some very interesting children. I have always made it a practice to see or find good in everyone and there were times when the good I found in a child's development was written into reports to parents and guardians, much to their delight.

By virtue of most of my career being in relation to children with special needs, I met some very special children who had very complex needs in their physical, emotional and communication development. One particular girl was an elective mute. Though I was aware of mutism, she was the first one I had worked with.

At school, she would go for hours, or even days, and not say a word and when she did it was only to her friend who then passed on her comment or request to the teacher. At home, she was different and would speak softly to her family but would rarely speak outside of the home and then only to the friend she trusted. She was a pretty girl, lovely in personality and she loved her school. Around her was an atmosphere of peace and calm and quiet.

In contrast, another young person I know was at the other extreme. He was so noisy and determined to be seen and heard, that we referred to him as the voice. Living in the Southeast of England at the time, for a day out we would sometimes go to Eastbourne. This is a town right on the coast where there is a lighthouse with a powerful foghorn.

This is needed especially when the coastal fog is so thick the light is unable to penetrate it and it then cannot do its job to warn shipping of the dangerous coast. Playfully, we joked that if the foghorn ever broke down, our young man could do the job very nicely and stand on Beachy Head shouting rocks!

The miracle we are now examining has both these extremes. There is uncanny and unnerving silence accompanying action, and shouting so loud that it contributed to an amazing outcome. Both are important extremes and both are used by God's people as strategies in this conquest.

For 40 years, the Israelites wandered in the wilderness, eating quail and manna (Exodus 16:11–12), and wearing clothes and shoes which didn't wear out (Deuteronomy 29:5). They didn't even develop foot problems as a nation despite all the hard walking, 'Nor did their feet become swollen' (Nehemiah 9:21).

On one occasion, water came out of a rock when struck by Moses with his staff (Exodus 17:1–7), on another the lifting of Moses' hands watching an army led by Joshua into battle, caused the Israelites to win (v8–13). So, despite a delayed journey to the Promised Land which took years when it should have taken days, God was with his people so miracles occurred when needed along the way.

The Israelites were given the land by God and the people wanted to return to it from their stay in Egypt. The delay was because the people didn't exercise faith until Joshua gave the lead. He was the assistant to Moses (Joshua 1:1) and accompanied him when he went up Mt. Sinai to receive the Ten Commandments (Exodus 24:13) and then he came down with him.[34]

Moses declared Joshua to be his successor, so when Moses died, Joshua took over the leadership of a vast number of people and kept moving forward with them by faith, towards the Promised Land. However, it was not a question of walking back into the land their ancestor Jacob left behind with his family and servants.

Much had changed in their absence and warlike tribes occupied the land. If they were going to re-possess their inheritance, they were going to have to fight for it. Joshua was the person right for the job: a leader, warrior and strategist and he listened to God.

His first major task was to lead the people over the river Jordan. Having travelled with Moses through the Red Sea he knew that if God did the miracle of parting the waters once he could do it again.

God gave Joshua firm instructions and promised to support him if he obeyed:

'No one will be able to stand against you all the days of your life. As I was with Moses, so I will be with you; I will never leave you nor forsake you. Be strong and courageous, because you will lead these people to inherit the land I swore to their ancestors to give them. Be strong and very courageous. Be careful to obey all the law my servant Moses gave you; do not turn from it to the right or to the left, that you may be successful wherever you go' (Joshua 1:5–7).

Joshua obeyed; he trusted God; the people trusted Joshua; the river was crossed (Joshua 3:17).

The second major task was to conquer the city of Jericho which stood at the gateway to the Promised Land of Canaan but the Amorite people there (Joshua 5:1) felt secure in their city surrounded by very thick and well-constructed walls,[35] and we read, 'Now the gates of Jericho were securely barred because of the Israelites. No-one went out and no-one came in' (Joshua 6:1).

Victory at Jericho really would prove that God was with his people and wanted them to win back and re-occupy Canaan. 'This was the land of milk and honey God had promised to Abraham over 500 years earlier (Deuteronomy 6:3, 32:49).'[36]

Pamela Palmer is a writer, chaplain, and the founder of upheldlife.com,[37] who makes the observation:

'The story of Joshua leading the Israelites to bring down the walls of Jericho is a powerful account that demonstrates the faithfulness and might of the LORD. This narrative is part of the fulfilment of the greater promise that God made to the Israelites that they indeed would enter the Promised Land.'

In education, it is always worthwhile taking children to visit places of interest where they could and should learn things first-hand. Staff used to call this *doing a recce* (reconnoitre). This was so that once we had children with lively, and sometimes challenging behaviour in public; we could anticipate what might go right as well as wrong before we actually got the children back to school.

For similar reasons, Joshua sends out his spies to assess Jericho before they cross the Jordan and his army attacks the city.

At night, the two spies crossed the Jordan, crept into the walled city of Jericho and hid at the house of Rahab, who was a prostitute. Visitors to her house would not immediately cause suspicion. Jericho had a double wall and her house was between the walls (Joshua 2:15).

Despite her lifestyle, Rahab had a personal faith in God and once she knew why the spies had come, she informed them of Jericho's panic:

'I know that the LORD has given this land to you and that a great fear of you has fallen on us so that all who live in this country are melting in fear because of you' (v9).

She helped the spies hide from the king's messengers, who visited her looking for them, and then the spies left out of her window using a scarlet rope down the outside wall. Before they left, Rahab demanded the spies affirm an oath since she swore not to give their plans away, and in turn, they vowed to spare Rahab and her family when the battle of Jericho occurred.

She agreed she would fasten the rope out her window (v18), so the invading Israelites would see it and keep her and her family safe. Wikipedia adds that the spies got all the positive encouragement they needed and, 'Discovered that the land was in fear of them and their God.'[38]

The battle strategy for taking Jericho is intriguing.[39] God gave Joshua a promise that they would win the battle and told them how to defeat Jericho and claim the city. For the first six days, the armed men were to march around the city once while the priests blew trumpets and carried the Ark of the Covenant.

They did this for six days. God concluded his instructions, 'On the seventh day, march round the city seven times, with the priests blowing the trumpets. When you hear them sound a long blast on the trumpets, make the whole army give a loud shout; then the wall of the city will collapse and the army will go up, everyone straight in' (Joshua 6:4–5).[40]

These instructions Joshua passed on to the people. Except for the seven trumpet-blowing priests accompanying the Ark which represented the visible presence of God, they were to walk around the city each day in silence, or at least, very quietly, 'Do not give the war cry, do not raise your voices' (v10a).

Then, Joshua gave a vital command:

'Do not say a word until the day I tell you to shout. Then shout!' (v10b)

God led the people. Joshua followed his instructions. The people followed Joshua and walked in faith.

The victory was secure:

'When the trumpets sounded, the army shouted, and at the sound of the trumpet (*the long blast of Joshua 6:5*), when the men gave a loud shout, the wall collapsed; so everyone charged straight in, and they took the city' (v20) (*Insertion mine*).

Bible Study Tools researchers tell us: 'Joshua assured them that by God's order, everyone in the city must be slain, except Rahab and her family. All items of silver, gold, bronze, and iron were to go into the Lord's depository.'[41]

As the city was being attacked, Joshua despatched the two spies to go into Jericho again, and Rahab and her family were led to safety (v22–23) and were the only ones spared (v25a).[42]

Final thoughts

[1] God spoke to Joshua. And because Joshua was in tune with God and took the time to listen and seek his direction, he heard clearly from God what to do (Joshua: 1:5–7 and 6:2–5).[43]

[2] Joshua obeyed God even when his commands didn't make sense, but he had learned from Moses that listening to God and obeying him brings victory (Exodus 14:22). Now, Joshua was faced with the Jordan to cross then Jericho to defeat and he went forward in obedience to God's instructions (Joshua 3:17 and 6:20). Each time the impossible happened.

[3] God had given the city of Jericho to the Israelites before they even began to march around its walls (Joshua 6:2, v16). The walls should have been impenetrable, and God did not instruct Joshua and his army to storm the city upon arrival, or when they were ready. It was when the people of God, by faith, followed the commands of God at the right time when he was ready, that the walls of Jericho fell down (v20).

[4] Joshua learned it was to be God's way and not by human reasoning (Isaiah 55:8–9).

[5] The power of God is supernatural, beyond understanding (Daniel 4:35). The Israelites had to learn to wait for God's timing which was seven days later. Meanwhile, they marched; they camped; they waited. Perhaps, some of the armed soldiers wondered, as they were marching around the walls, if this really was the way to achieve victory over Jericho?

Maybe some thought it would be best to win the city with a proven military strategy. The walls of Jericho fell instantly because of the people's submission to God's will and obedience to his instructions (Joshua 6:2–17a). The NT links success with faith.

In commenting on this story, the writer to the Hebrews tells us, 'By faith, the walls of Jericho fell, after the people had marched around them for seven days' (Hebrews 11:30).

[6] The fall of Jericho tells us that God is faithful to his promises (Joshua 6:2, v20).

[7] Joshua and the Israelites carried out the commands of God and conquered Jericho because the occupants were an enemy trying to keep the Israelites out of the Promised Land they had been given (v1–2).

[8] Joshua knew that he and his army had to act decisively in accordance with God's wishes and remember whom he was saving. James in his NT letter uses the example of Rahab whose lifestyle left much to be desired but whose faith was in place (James 2:25). When the attack came, Rahab hung out the scarlet cord in faith, as agreed with the spies (Joshua 2:21), for rescue and protection (Joshua 6:22–23).

I trust that despite our imperfections, we display the scarlet cord of faith in God for rescue and protection from sin and opposition from the Enemy through circumstances or people!

Questions to consider:

1. Was the survival of the Israelites in the wilderness for 40 years because of God's provision or because of chance?
2. Is it possible to be a person of ill repute, and be a Christian?
3. Were the experienced soldiers right to trust Joshua with untried battle techniques and strategies?

Conflict Days

'Go in the strength you have' (Judges 6:14b).
Full story: (Judges 6:1–23, 7, 8:22–28, v35)

As a teacher getting ready to teach a class, a headteacher forming an agenda for a staff meeting or a parent planning a holiday for the family and thinking about accommodation, travel and how much we have to spend, I know careful preparation needs to be made. Without the preparation, there cannot be a successful experience and little will be achieved.

I know from experience that it is possible to have a task to address and not feel adequate. It is possible to have the twin challenges of being unprepared and not being equal to the task. I think we will come to see Gideon was like this.

Gideon appears in three chapters of the OT book of Judges (6–8), and he was the fifth judge to lead Israel. He became an outstanding warrior but the way he won a major battle against the Midianites is the next miracle to be examined. He follows the only female judge we are told about, Deborah.

Deborah was a busy woman. We read, 'Now Deborah, a prophet, the wife of Lappidoth, was leading Israel at that time. She held court under the Palm of Deborah between Ramah and Bethel in the hill country of Ephraim, and the Israelites went up to her to have their disputes decided' (Judges 4:4–5).

Pastor Pam Otten of Renew Church, Wisconsin tells us, 'Deborah was a woman of great wisdom, revelation, and discernment. She also had a prophetic gift, including knowing the times and seasons of the LORD. She clearly heard the voice of the LORD.'[44]

After Deborah's bravery and success in battle and in leadership we read, 'Then, the land had peace for 40 years' (Judges 5:31c).

But the peace was not to last, and the faith of the Israelites trusting God to lead them was not to last.

We are told at the start of the next chapter that, 'The Israelites did evil in the eyes of the LORD, and for seven years he gave them into the hands of the Midianites' (Judges 6:1).

The Israelites settled into agriculture and rural living, and as the Pastor of the First Baptist Church, Gulf Shores, Alabama, expresses it, 'Everything's coming up roses. And as it tends to happen to us all in such times, Israel forgot God. They became self-sufficient. They didn't need God. So, the LORD shook things up by rousing an enemy against them to show them how hard life can be without him.'[45]

The people felt utterly defeated. They hid in strongholds and caves and whenever they planted crops and reared animals, the Midianites, Amalekites and other nomadic groups came regularly and destroyed their efforts.

Wikipedia says of God's people, 'God chastised them by delivering them into the hands of the Midianties. They worshipped their own images reflected in the water, and they were stricken with dire poverty. They could not bring so much as a meal offering, the offering of the poor.'[46]

It was in desperation, and sadly, perhaps, as a last resort after all else had failed, they cried out to God for help. God, therefore, sent an unnamed prophet to tell them they were suffering because they had forsaken God and were not listening to him.

Following this, an angel is despatched by God to visit Gideon, whom he knew to be a man of faith and tell him that he had been chosen to do something about the sorry state the Israelites were in. The angel found him secretly threshing wheat and hiding it from the enemy. He was in a winepress and that may well have been underground. For Gideon, that was a place of safety.

Surprisingly, the angel addressed him with an unexpected title saying, 'The LORD is with you, mighty warrior' (v12) (*Emphasis mine*).

Though he was hiding from the enemy, and was from a poor family from which a leader wouldn't normally emerge, he reacted with humility. Others around him felt defeated but Gideon didn't. He was hiding in a winepress where you wouldn't expect to see someone threshing wheat, to be cautious, but he was actually acting with courage because at least he was doing something whilst other people were starving and just hiding away (v2).

He spoke to the angel questioning where God was if all these problems were happening to the Israelites. He pointed out that in wilderness travelling days miracles happened but because things were going wrong and there was an absence of miracles he and the people felt God had abandoned them.

The angel,[47] now referred to as The LORD, addressed him face to face (v22), and said, 'Go in the strength you have and save Israel out of Midian's hand. Am I not sending you?' (v14) In this we have the key words for this miracle: **'Go in the strength you have.'**

This tells us that the angel and the LORD are synonymous on this occasion. As the angel speaks with God's authority, it is as the LORD speaking. As God commissions Gideon he empowers him by the words of his command. Gideon was not to rely on others but to believe he could bring about the overthrow of enemies by his faith and trust in God, and by his own intelligence, skill and courage.

Gideon spoke very firmly to the angel and tried to point out that he didn't have the right background to meet the calling but God, the angel, simply promised him success in battle. Gideon knew the power of God and the history of Israel. He then looked for further confirmation that God meant what he said, so next he prepared his offering to God.

The angel reacted by touching it with the tip of his staff, causing fire to come out of the rock and burn it up, and then he suddenly disappeared (v21). Because he saw God, at least in the angel, Gideon thought he would probably die, but God assured him that he would not die.[48]

Gideon was beginning to understand the messenger and what was being required of him. His first big task was to deal with idolatry symbolised on the altar to Baal, which had become the evil described at the start of chapter six (v1).

He therefore tore down the altar to Baal and built one to the LORD God, 'And called it The LORD is Peace—' ('Jehovah-shalom' KJV) (v24).

Meanwhile, the Midianites and other tribes joined forces again to threaten and then attack Israel. Gideon was now ready to act. 'Then the Spirit of the LORD came on Gideon, and he blew a trumpet, summoning the Abiezrites to follow him' (v34).

He, then, gathered more men to fight from three more tribes of Israel to join the army he was forming.

Gideon was still not totally convinced of God's will so he then requested of God two further miracles involving a fleece on two consecutive nights with opposite outcomes. The first morning, he woke to his fleece covered in dew, but the surrounding ground was dry. The second morning, he woke to his fleece being dry and the ground being wet (v36–40). This happened. Gideon was now sure he had understood God and went forward towards battle (Judges 7:1).

At this point, there was an issue with the size of his 32,000-strong army. God wanted to receive the glory for victory and not Gideon and his army (v2), so the army had to be reduced in stages. This would be easier for Gideon to accept than if he was told in advance that he would have a tiny army and have to march against a much larger one.

David Peach, multi-linguist and director of Deaf Ministries, Tennessee, adds, 'Gideon said that the men who were afraid to go to battle were welcome to return home. It may have been disheartening for Gideon to see 22,000 men turn around and walk away. But Gideon was left with 10,000 brave men' (v3).[49] This was further reduced to 300 watchful and brave men (v7), to face a mighty enemy of 135,000 (Judges 8:10).

Gideon was now preparing for battle in practical terms and was listening to God, his LORD for direction. In the night, God knew that Gideon needed further encouragement so God spoke to him again (Judges 7:9).

Gideon followed instructions and took his servant Purah to the Midianite camp to listen to what the enemy was saying. Two soldiers were talking and one told the other of his dream. They interpreted the details as Gideon being victorious against them in battle. Gideon was so thankful to hear that and he worshipped God on the spot before returning to his small army. He devised a battle plan with three companies of 100. Each person was given a ram's horn trumpet and flaming torch hidden in a clay jar (v16). (We are not told that his army had any weapons!)

Gideon told them to copy him as a role model. 'Watch me,' he told them. 'Follow my lead. When I get to the edge of the camp, do exactly as I do. When I and all who are with me blow our trumpets, then from all round the camp blow yours and shout, "For the LORD and for Gideon"' (v17–18).

Gideon was ready in body, mind and spirit. He had a select company of 300 warriors. The odds were 450 to one against him. The overwhelming advantage he had was that God was with him and was his strength.

That is why we read that God said, 'Go in the strength you have and save Israel—' (Judges 6:14).

Gideon and his company of 100 men led the way and enacted the battle plan. At the change of guard in the Midianite camp, the enemy was suddenly surrounded by shouting and the smashing of clay jars to reveal flaming torches which were inside them (Judges 7:19–20). This suggested to the Midianites by sound and sight that a very large force was attacking them. They had no idea of the size of the opposing army and were in total panic and in leaderless uncoordinated disarray.

In the darkness and in their stress, they rushed about killing each other. They didn't know how many thousand soldiers were in their camp. In fact, there were none! The Israelites at this point held their ground surrounding the camp. The Midianites broke through this thin cordon and fled (v21). There were so many in the enemy army to catch and destroy that the Israelites called for assistance from the Ephraimites.

The surviving enemy soldiers from the camp ran away right into the home area of Gideon's 30,000 soldiers he had sent home. So, those soldiers joined in the slaughter of the Midianites (v23–25).

Gideon's success was so appreciated that the whole nation wanted him to be their king, but Gideon insisted, 'The LORD will rule over you' (Judges 8:23b).

As a reward, however, he asks for and receives the gold earrings from the plunder worn by the defeated enemy. He later fashioned some of the jewellery into an ephod which, sadly, after Gideon's death, the people soon used for idolatrous purposes (v24–27). This suggests an error on Gideon's part in not foreseeing what a snare it could be.

David Peach rounds off his summary of the story, 'During his pursuit of the enemy armies, Gideon had trouble from some of the tribes of Israel that would not give food to Gideon's army so that they could continue to fight. Gideon came back and slew those uncooperative men (*to avenge the death of his own brothers* [see: Judges 8:19–21]). The fear of Gideon and his men was stabilising enough so that Israel lived in peace and worshipped God for the next 40 years until Gideon's death' (v28, v32) (*Insertion mine*).[50]

His life changed after his military exploits as he moved from leading as a warrior to leading as a judge in more settled times. Sadly, as soon as he died in old age, the Israelites again turned to worship the false god Baal Berith and ignored the family and faith of Gideon and all the good he had done (3–35). However, Gideon was the right man at the right time to lead the people into faith and victory and so is mentioned in the NT *Hall of Fame* (Hebrews 11:32).

Final thoughts

[1] God uses tough times to get the attention of his people (Judges 6:1–6). Idolatry was rife, so for seven years, the Israelites suffered at the hands of the Midianites who were extremely powerful and oppressed them mercilessly. Every year around harvest time, they would invade Israel. They came in like locusts, ravaging the land. What they couldn't carry with them they destroyed. Through all this, God was disciplining those whom he loved (Proverbs 3:11–12).

The people had a painful and tough existence which should have turned them to God as the one who allowed it and could do something about it. C. S. Lewis (1898–1963) explained the pain used to get their attention as, 'God's megaphone.'[51]

[2] God did respond to the need and the eventual desperate request from his people, but they had to make the request before he acted to free the people from Midianite oppression (Judges 6:6).

[3] God in his mercy and love for his people, acted decisively in two ways. First, he sent a prophet to explain why the people were in their current predicament. Second, he sent an angel with the authority of the LORD himself to empower Gideon to lead in battle. Gideon had a mixture of courage and caution.

God addressed him as a 'mighty warrior' (v12), which was true under the surface, and told him to go forward in the strength he already possessed (v14). He had all the gifts and qualities with which to serve God and his people but he was cautious and didn't have the confidence at first.

[4] Gideon was a man with deep-seated courage, who was learning to hear from God and learning to trust him, but he needed three miracles from God before he moved forward in confidence (v17–21, v36–38 and v39–40).[52]

[5] Gideon was re-directed in his priorities and actions by God. He went from hiding in a winepress to brave leadership of a heavily outnumbered small band of soldiers. The change happened because he believed God who promised to be with him telling him, 'Go in the strength you have…Am I not sending you…I will be with you' (Judges 6:14, v16) and promised him victory before the battle even begun (Judges 7:7).

Gideon had now heard correctly and in the night woke up his elite soldiers with the words 'Get up! The LORD has given the Midianite camp into your hands' (v15b).

[6] The planning was perfect and led to victory. God organised the reduction in troop numbers to the number he wanted. Gideon organised the strategic battle details. As with Joshua at Jericho, faith and works came together, as the NT James teaches using Jericho's Rahab as an example (James 2:25–26).

[7] Gideon refused to accept to be king of the Israelites at their request and knew that was God's chosen position for himself with his people, and not Gideon's. God was King and Gideon remained as judge.[53] What Gideon did request, however, was some of the plunder from the defeated and then slaughtered Midianites.

With the earrings, he made an ephod garment. After Gideon's death, this was worshipped by the Israelites who resorted back to idolatry and still did not exercise faith in their lives and worship.

Perhaps Gideon should not have created this garment (Judges 8:22–27).

[8] Success is determined by God's power not that of people.

I trust we know that success comes from God and allow him to work miracles in our lives. We may then see him in our experience as we learn to trust him by faith.

Questions to consider:

1. Would we say Gideon was brave or afraid when the angel met him in Judges 6:12?
2. Was Gideon right to request a second fleece after the first in Judges 6:36–40?
3. Is vengeance ever justified as in Judges 8:19–21?

6 David

'The battle is the LORD's—' (1 Samuel 17:47b)
Full story: (1 Samuel 17)

There is a song written by Arthur Arnott, a Salvation Army Officer, I have sung at Sunday School and taught to children with actions over the years:

'Only a boy called David, only a rippling brook.

Only a boy called David, but five little stones he took.

And one little stone went into the sling and the sling went round and round,

One little stone went into the sling and the sling went round and round.

Round and round and round and round and round and round and round,

One little stone went up, up, up,

And the giant came tumbling down.'[54]

The song embodies amazing truths and this victory over the enemy giant is the next miracle for our study.

David was the youngest of Jesse's 12 sons, his great-grandmother was Ruth, a Moabite, who accompanied her Jewish mother-in-law back to Israel from Moab after both their husbands had died. Ruth's faith in God and devotion to Naomi are detailed in the OT book bearing her name. David was a strong shepherd boy, skilled with a sling and was an accomplished musician who, one day, would become king.

The Philistines were probably the Sea People who left the coastal areas of Greece, Crete, Asia Minor, and the Aegean Islands and settled on the eastern Mediterranean coast. They dominated the region including the five fortified cities of Gaza, Gath, Ekron,

Ashkelon and Ashdod. From 1200 to about 1000 BC, the Philistines were Israel's principal enemies.

As a people, they were skilled in using a forge to make iron tools and had the ability to construct impressive chariots. With these chariots of war, they dominated the coastal plains but they were ineffective in the mountainous regions of central Israel. This put them at a disadvantage with their Israelite neighbours who were farmers at this time but ready for war when necessary.

The Philistines marched against King Saul, who reigned 1043–1004 BC, and the Israelites; they camped at Ephes Dammim. The Israelite army gathered nearby in the valley of Elah and got ready for a fight. Each day, the battle lines were drawn but there was no action.

The two armies were on hilltops with a valley between them. The sides of the valley were very steep. Whoever made the first move into the valley and uphill would have a strong disadvantage and probably suffer a great loss. Both sides were waiting for the other to attack first.

Instead of a full-scale battle, with the loss of many good soldiers, the Philistines came up with a simple plan. That was for their champion to fight the Israelites champion and the winner would take over the conquered nation.[55] Twice a day, morning and evening for 40 days, Goliath, the champion of the Philistines challenged the Israelites to appoint their champion to fight him. Everyone was afraid of him as he seemed invincible. This gave Saul a particular problem. The colloquialism, "size matters" is appropriate here!

Height and strength were important, and as Saul was about *seven feet six*, 'He was higher than any of the people from his shoulders and upward' (1 Samuel 10:23 KJV).

So, being the king and the tallest Israelite, he should have not only led his people into battle but also, as the champion of his people,[56] should have fought Goliath, but he felt intimidated by the sheer size and power of Goliath who was six cubits and a span, or *nine feet ten* inches tall (1 Samuel 17:4).[57]

No Hebrew soldier dared face this giant. He had very substantial armour weighing 5,000 shekels (58 Kg or 128 pounds). He was incredibly strong but his armour was so heavy he needed an assistant to carry his shield to protect his front (v41). Not only was he causing terror by his appearance, but his shouted words insulted and defied the God of Israel (v45).[58]

David's three oldest brothers out of eight, were soldiers in the army but David had to stay at home because he was the youngest brother and had to look after his father's sheep. One day, his father, Jesse, sent the teenage David to the front lines with food for his brothers. Without complaint, David obeyed his father (v17–20).[59]

There he heard Goliath mocking Israel and God. This greatly annoyed David so he volunteered to Saul to fight Goliath. David persuaded Saul but he tried on and then took off again Saul's armour which, fitting Saul's great size, was too large for David to wear and he certainly wouldn't be able to fight in it.

'I cannot go in these,' he said to Saul, 'because I am not used to them. So, he took them off' (v39b).

David resorted to what he was good at; taking on the challenges as he did fight a lion and bear, when they attacked his sheep, in his normal shepherd's clothes and using only his sling. He gathered from a stream five smooth stones which he knew would fly well. He took one for each of Goliath's brothers as well in case he also had to fight them![60]

David convinced Saul he was equal to the task of killing Goliath and so Saul let him try and watched what would happen (v55). David knew that he could fight Goliath even though he had never faced a giant in the past. He used the past victories to give confidence that God would continue to work in and through him (v34–37).

He assures Saul by saying, 'The LORD who rescued me from the paw of the lion and the paw of the bear will rescue me from the hand of this Philistine—' (v37a).

At least, it got Saul out of his dilemma and saved face with his people. David and Goliath confronted each other. Goliath had his armour and assistant to help protect him. He despised David (v42) as if to say, '*Is this the best you can come up with?*'

Then, he cursed David "by his gods" (v43). David had his staff, his sling, his stones and his deep-seated trust in God.

He said to the Philistine, 'You come against me with sword and spear and javelin, but I come against you in the name of the LORD Almighty' (v45).

And we encounter here our key words for this miracle, **'The battle is the LORD's** and he will give all of you into our hands' (v47b).

David was using his experience of protecting sheep[61] and was determined that no one was going to insult the LORD his God. He was sure with God he would win and that all the Philistines would be defeated.

To David, God's honour and name were at stake, 'And the whole world will know that there is a God in Israel' (v46b).

As Goliath lumbered forward, David ran to him, then took action in a split-second spotting a gap in Goliath's armour, before Goliath had time to see what was coming!

Wikipedia concludes:

'David hurls a stone from his sling and hits Goliath in the centre of his forehead, Goliath falls on his face to the ground, and David cuts off his head. The Philistines flee and are pursued by the Israelites, 'To the entrance of Gath and to the gates of Ekron—' (v52). David puts the weapons of Goliath in his own tent and takes the head to Jerusalem.'[62]

The Philistine's retreat gave the Israelites all the encouragement they needed to chase after them right to the enemy's city gates including Gath where their champion came from. This would be the height of humiliation for the Philistines.

Saul rightly wanted to honour David, a brave young warrior, who had done what Saul couldn't do, and give him the promised wealth, a bride and freedom from taxes (v25).

To Saul, David's pedigree was important, and as Mary Fairchild, a Christian writer, editor, and full-time minister with Learn Religion adds, 'When asked by Saul who he is, he says he is the son of Jesse and from Bethlehem.'[63]

David had been anointed (1 Samuel: 16:12–13) as the next king of Israel (1004–971 BC) but was still a boy, probably a teenager and was waiting to take over from Saul.

Final thoughts

[1] In this account of David and Goliath, we see David as a young man acting in obedience. He obeyed his father Jesse; he obeyed God when prompted to fight Goliath; he obeyed Saul when asked to put on the armour—before discarding it.

[2] When David arrived in the camp, he was hurt to hear the language Goliath was using against 'The armies of the living God' (1 Samuel 17:26b).

He must have seen his people fleeing in fear, but he reacted by showing there was a cause to fight for.

[3] When David heard that God would gain the victory, he wanted to be part of it (v26).

[4] The armour of Saul rejected by David represented human strength. David couldn't wear someone else's armour but relied on God for his strength.[64] Paul writing to the Christians at Ephesus encouraged them to, 'Put on the full armour of God, so that you can take your stand against the devil's schemes' (Ephesians 6:11). David and the Christians in Ephesus learned to trust God's strength.

[5] The Philistines turned and ran when they saw their giant hero killed. Israel had won the battle because of a boy who had faith and trusted God![65]

[6] The Biblical account of David and Goliath is one of the most popular stories from Scripture. It is a lesson of courage, faith, and overcoming what seems impossible.[66]

[7] By his victory over Goliath which led to total victory by the Israelites over the Philistines, David demonstrated that he was worthy to become Israel's next King.

[8] David was able to look at the giant from a different perspective. He looked at the problem from God's point of view. He knew 'The battle is the LORD's—' (1 Samuel 17:47).

[9] David Peach, Director of Deaf Ministries, Tennessee, points out that 'David had already demonstrated his great musical talent in the previous chapters of 1 Samuel. But that very public and prestigious skill of playing the harp did no good in this situation. What won the day was David's ability that was honed whilst being an unknown shepherd boy who dedicated his life to living with sheep.'[67]

[10] David was an ancestor of Jesus Christ, who was often called *The Son of David* such as in Matthew (1:1). Perhaps, the greatest thing said about David was that he was raised up by God who sought out a man after his own heart (1 Samuel 13:14 and Act 13:22). He is also listed in the Hall of Faith (Hebrews 11:32).

When we face a giant problem or impossible situation, we should stop for a minute and re-focus. That way we see things more clearly from God's perspective.

Questions to consider:

1. Is there a Goliath threatening us?
2. If people curse and blaspheme our God, what should we do about it?
3. In what ways will the armour of God help us with daily living, as in Ephesians 6:10?

Prophetic Days

7 Elijah

'My father! My father! The chariots and horsemen of Israel'
(2 Kings 2:12).

Full story: (2 Kings 2:1–12)

If I wrote a recent CV (Résumé), I would include details of my own education. I would list my professional positions. I may mention my links with special needs in the UK and several other countries. I would inform readers of my family situation and I would give my interests including involvement in the community.

I may list sporting and recreational interests and I could list activities in which I have served as a Christian. And so, the CV would unfold. I imagine I wouldn't speak about miracles and it would not be usual to speak of God directing me in my decision-making in my professional life. In many ways, my life would be unremarkable.

If we attempted to write a CV for Elijah, it would in contrast be very remarkable. David Sandford, a freelance writer summarises the prophet's life:

'At Elijah's word, kings trembled, the rains stopped, a jug of oil never ran dry, a boy was raised from the dead, fire fell from the sky, revival broke out, and hundreds of idolatrous prophets of Baal were executed.'[68]

Elijah is one of the most interesting and colourful people in the Bible, and God used him during an important time in Israel's history to oppose a wicked king and bring revival to the land. Elijah's ministry marked the beginning of the end of Baal worship in Israel. He is considered to be one of the greatest prophets and is linked to many unique miracles in the OT. Further to Sandford's list above, we could add:

- Causing rain and dew to cease in Israel for three years (1 Kings 17:1).
- Being fed by ravens sent by God (1 Kings 17:4).
- Multiplying a widow's grain and oil (1 Kings 17:16).
- Raising that widow's son from the dead (1 Kings 17:22).
- Calling fire from heaven on top of Mount Carmel (1 Kings 18:38).
- Causing it to rain again after three years of drought (1 Kings 18:1, v45).
- Fasting from food for 40 days whilst travelling to Mount Horeb (1 Kings 19:8).
- Prophesying that Ahab's sons would all be destroyed (1 Kings 21:21).
- Prophesying that Jezebel would be eaten by dogs (1 Kings 21:23).
- Prophesying that Jehoram would die a horrible death from a bowel disease (2 Chronicles 21:19).
- Prophesying that Ahaziah would die of his illness (2 Kings 1:4).
- Calling fire from heaven to destroy two groups of 51 soldiers (2 Kings 1:10, v12).
- Parting the river Jordan while accompanied by Elisha (2 Kings 2:8).
- Promising that Elisha would receive a double portion of Elijah's spirit (2 Kings 2:10).
- Being caught up to heaven with a chariot of fire and horses of fire (2 Kings 2:11).

Elijah continues to be held in high esteem by the Jews, and a special position in their nation. Sarah Gray, a journalist with The Global News Agency, writing for Time magazine explains that

Elijah is remembered each year at the annual Passover in traditional Jewish homes.[69]

Elijah's key role in Israel's history is why he is one of two OT figures who appear with Jesus, speaking about Jesus' departure from Earth, on the Mount of Transfiguration: Moses representing the Law and Elijah the Prophets (Matthew 17:3–13, Mark 9:4–13 and Luke 9:30–33). He is mentioned 29 times in six NT books, including the Gospels, Romans, James and Revelation, mostly in relation to his faith and miracles.

It has been calculated that Elijah was born in 900 BC and died in 849 BC,[70] but scholars differ on these dates.[71] Most agree, however, that he ministered around the middle of the C 9th.

We read of him in 1 and 2 Kings (1 Kings 17–19, v21, 2 Kings 1–2), and meet him again in Malachi, who writes a little after 433 BC, where John the Baptist is promised (Malachi 3:1), then, detailed in the lifestyle and appearance of Elijah in the last words of the OT (Malachi 4:5–6). This statement was widely held in Jewish Intertestamental literature to mean that Elijah himself would return in person and announce the arrival of the LORD.

Elijah is an ordinary man but was called to an extraordinary position in his life, teaching, and faith. At the end of his life, which is different from all other people except for Enoch, he went to heaven without dying (Genesis 5:24 and Hebrews 11:5). In relation to his background, he was from Tishbe in Gilead. We know nothing of his parents, or of his age when he began ministry.

His name stems from a Hebrew expression meaning *Jehovah is my God*, from the Hebrew words El (God) and Yah (Jehovah). He was devoted to the LORD his God and was not afraid to speak for him to anyone as God led him. Except for a prophecy against King Jehoram of the Southern Kingdom of Judah, all his ministry was to the Northern Kingdom of Israel during the reign of King Ahab.

Robert Bradshaw, librarian at Spurgeon's College, London, notes:

The reign of Ahab was a dark hour for Israel. Not only had he and his father Omri exceeded the sins of all the kings that preceded them in their worship of Jeroboam's golden calves, but he had also married Jezebel, daughter of Ethbaal the priest-king of the Sidonians' (1 Kings 16:25–26, v30–33).[72] This marriage was supposed to cement an alliance between the two nations of Sidon (the Canaanites) and Israel, but it failed to do so and Jezebel brought with her idol worship.

We see Elijah fearlessly defending the worship of Jehovah, his LORD God, over that of the Canaanite deity Baal whom many Israelites were worshipping and so causing God to be very displeased.[73]

King Ahab didn't look kindly on Elijah, and on one occasion when they met, King Ahab greeted him and we read:

'When he saw Elijah, he said to him, "Is that you, you troubler of Israel?"

"I have not made trouble for Israel", Elijah replied. "But you and your father's family have. You have abandoned the LORD's commands and have followed the Baals"' (I Kings 18:17–18).

Kevin Smyth, Professor of Scripture at Dublin University, adds that Elijah's words, 'Show that more is at stake than simply allotting to divinities their particular spheres of influence. The true question is whether Yahweh or Baal is God.'[74]

Elijah led a company of prophets (2 Kings 2:3) and these were later under the leadership of Elisha as his successor.

Wikipedia adds:

'As told in the Hebrew Bible, Elijah's challenge is bold and direct. Baal was the Canaanite god responsible for rain, thunder, lightning, and dew. Elijah thus, when he initially announces the drought, not only challenges Baal on behalf of God himself, but he also challenges Jezebel, her priests, Ahab and the people of Israel.'[75]

Baal and Asherah were introduced into worship by Jezebel, who was a Phoenician princess, and as she had a strong influence over Ahab, this accounts for her hatred of Elijah when Baal and the prophets of Baal were defeated.

According to David Mandel, a Jewish Bible scholar, 'She introduced in Israel the Phoenician pagan cult of the god Baal, a development that was bitterly opposed by the prophet Elijah.'[76]

Robert Bradshaw adds, 'When the direct confrontation with Baal priests on Carmel finally comes about it is Yahweh, not Baal, who answers; first with fire (1 Kings 18:36–38), and then with rain (v41–45).'[77]

As the Society for Old Testament Study makes clear, 'The central feature of Elijah's ministry is his strong opposition to the kings of Israel and to the worship of the Canaanite god Baal, promoted by them. In the course of that opposition, Elijah slaughters pagan prophets (1 Kings 18:40) and announces the end of Ahab's dynasty (1 Kings 21:21–22).'[78]

The last miracle of all involving Elijah in the OT is when he is caught up by God and taken to heaven. This is the incident at the end of Elijah's life on Earth which is the subject of our present miracle.

Elijah's entry into Israelite daily politics, worship and life generally is both abrupt and dramatic. His departure is similar. He has times of highs and lows in his life; great victory over people and circumstances as well as times of great fear and depression. He stands up to a wicked and cruel king with great confidence but becomes defeated by his wife the queen who threatens to kill him.

On one occasion, God sends an angel to revive him (1 Kings 19:5), as he is feeling so low. He anointed kings and appointed his successor, Elisha (v15–16), and though he thought he was the only person in Israel remaining faithful to God, God pointed out to him there were 7,000 others who were also faithful.

Despite being involved in a miracle-filled life, James, the stepbrother of Jesus, describes him as being a normal human being but having great faith and devotion to believing God would answer his prayers, 'Elijah was a human being, even as we are. He prayed earnestly that it would not rain, and it did not rain on the land for three and a half years. Again, he prayed, and the heavens gave rain, and the earth produced its crops' (James 5:17–18).

We must now look at the details of our miracle and consider the question: Why did Elijah not die? 1 Kings ends with the death of Ahab in battle (1 Kings 22:40), and his 22-year-old son Ahaziah succeeded him (1 Kings 22:51, 2 Kings 8:26).

We now move into 2 Kings and find Ahaziah falls from his roof and thinks he might die so he despatched servants to enquire of the idol god Baal, the likely result of his injuries. The LORD God was not pleased and sent an angel to tell Elijah to intercept this mission and ask why they were consulting an idol when the true God was present in Israel.

The answer to Ahaziah's faithless question could have been different had he turned to God, but is now very serious, 'Therefore this is what the LORD says, "You will not leave the bed you are lying on. You will certainly die!"' (2 Kings 1:4)

The servants returned to the king with the sad news from a stranger and the king worked out from the description that it was Elijah that they met on the way. The king was unhappy with the news, as you would expect, and so despatched 51 soldiers to round up Elijah and bring him to the king.

The company with their captain found Elijah and found him unwilling to come from the top of the hill where he was relaxing. Elijah's response was to call down fire from heaven and kill all 51. The king found out and despatched a second group and the same thing happened to them.

The third group of 50 and their captain were despatched but this captain was much more caring towards his company of soldiers and humbly begged Elijah for their lives to be spared. God noted this respect towards Elijah, so Elijah went with them to the king. However, his message was the same, Ahaziah was going to die because he was not prepared to show faith in God.

We now see that Elijah had completed his life's tasks and in the next chapter, 'The LORD was about to take Elijah up to heaven in a whirlwind' (2 Kings 2:12) as he and his assistant, Elisha left Gilgal on their way to Bethel. Elisha begged to stay with his master and the company of Elijah's prophets knew what was about to happen so they warned Elisha his master was about to leave him. This happened three times, testing Elisha's resolve.

He still wanted to stay with his master and they went on to Jericho and then to the Jordan. At the river, Elijah used his cloak to strike the water and it parted so they could cross the river on dry ground.

Elijah knew the time for his departure had come and agreed to Elisha's request, 'Let me inherit a double portion of your spirit' (2 Kings 2:10).

The double portion enables Elisha to inherit the priestly office (Deuteronomy 21:17).

Elijah had the authority to confer this so he said he would if Elisha saw him leave, otherwise it would not be conferred. They walked and talked and suddenly a chariot of fire pulled by horses of fire swept down between them in a whirlwind and took Elijah to heaven.

He left his cloak behind. 'Elisha saw this and cried out, **"My father! My father! The chariots and horsemen of Israel!"** And Elisha saw him no more' (2 Kings 2:12).

In this, we have the key words for this miracle. Elisha was saying the nation of Israel had lost its strength and power which it had by Elijah's presence. But this was now transferred to Elisha who accepted the leadership and authority straight away by striking the river again to cross back over the Jordan without getting wet! (2 Kings 2:14)

Elisha's ministry had begun.

Final thoughts

[1] Elijah ranks equal to Moses as one of the most dramatic prophets and as one of the key Bible characters who knew and honoured God. A widow concluded, 'You are a man of God...the word of the LORD from your mouth is truth' (1 Kings 17:24).

[2] James says that 'Elijah was as human as we are' (James 5:17). He had his faults and was terrified when Jezebel threatened to kill him (1 Kings 19:2), and he knew the depths of depression (v4), but he had human feelings and compassion when those qualities were needed when he was providing for a widow (1 Kings 17:16, v22).

[3] He was fearless in speaking the truth to kings and priests (1 Kings 18:18, v27).

[4] As already mentioned, it is not clear in the Bible why Elijah didn't die but was taken straight up to heaven. It was the way Enoch also went to heaven. Hebrews commends Enoch for his faith as 'One who pleased God' (Hebrews 11:5).

Elijah quite surprisingly is not mentioned in Hebrews 11 by name, but he is included in the words, and the prophets (v32), and is one of the people in the general statement, 'They went about in sheepskins and goatskins, destitute, persecuted and ill-treated' (v37).

I wonder if the way Elijah lived 'on the edge' (to quote a common idiom), was the way God chose for him to depart from the Earth. A normal death would be almost out of character!

[5] In the end, it is impossible to be sure why Elijah received the honour of not dying, but it shows us something encouraging.

The fact that God honoured Elijah in spite of his doubts reminds us that in the end, God will decide our legacy, and by his grace how he will provide for us and what he will allow to happen to us.

God loves us all and may decide to use us in unexpected ways. Elijah was able to challenge people with the words, 'If the LORD is God, follow him; but if Baal is God, follow him' (1 Kings 18:21b).

The choice is clear-cut.

[6] The website Got Questions has a useful conclusion in its article on Elijah: 'As was true for Elijah when we focus on the tumult of life in this world, we can get our eyes off of the LORD and become discouraged. God does display himself in mighty works of power and judgment such as wind, fire, and earthquakes, but he also relates with us intimately and personally, such as in the quiet whisper.'[79]

It was when Jezebel threatened the life of Elijah that he ran away in great fear and God met him not in great drama but by a whisper (1 Kings 19:11–12). Based on these verses, W. Garrett Horder (1841–1922), a Congregational Church minister,[80] wrote his lovely hymn in 1844, *Dear Lord and Father of Mankind*. The hymn concludes:

'Let sense be dumb, let flesh retire,
Speak through the earthquake, wind, and fire,
O still, small voice of calm,
O still, small voice of calm.'[81]
God was in the quiet whisper.

[7] Elijah may seem to be a stubborn and dramatic prophet who cared mostly about self-preservation. However, this is not how the Jews through the ages have understood these stories. Instead, he comes to play an important role in Jewish and Christian traditions and is seen as a man of faith, prayer and high principles and is

devoted to the LORD his God (Malachi 4:5, Mark 9:4 and James 5:17–18).

[8] Jesus endorsed the importance of Elijah by having a public conversation with him (and Moses), at his Transfiguration at which Elijah was representative of all the OT prophets. The three of them discussed the departure of Jesus from Earth back to his Father in heaven after completing his work of redemption on Earth.[82]

Just after the start of John's ministry, when that of Jesus started, he said, 'All the Prophets and the Law prophesied until John. And if you are willing to accept it, he is the Elijah who was to come' (Matthew 11:13–14).[83]

Whether in victory or despair, we can trust the LORD to bless us, guide us and use us in his service. This is sometimes in miraculous and unexpected ways.

Questions to consider:

1. If we had to become Prime Minister, name one quality we could put on a c.v. and bring to the post.
2. James 5:17 said Elijah was like us. Are we like him?
3. Is it right for a Christian to be depressed?

8 Jonah

'Salvation comes from the LORD' (Jonah 2:9C).

Full story: (Jonah 1–4)

At secondary school, I was mostly a good pupil and did as I was told. In P.E., I was particularly good at running short-distance races, long jump and throwing things such as a cricket ball, javelin, discus or putting the shot. I was quite good at all sports, but one I was reasonable at I hated.

In 1963, there was an exceptionally cold winter, the coldest in the UK for 200 years,[84] but I still had to do cross-country running. The teacher was young and a fitness fanatic and seemed to me and my friendship group that he had a mean streak which made us all change into tee shirts and shorts and run a rugged and steep course every week. *Week after week!*

I liked school too much to consider missing on cross-country days, so with my friends, I hatched a plan to shave about a mile off our three-mile course through a brown field site of bomb craters left from the Second World War enemy bombing of our heavily industrialised area of South Yorkshire. We simply took a shortcut and laid in wait and then joined the pack of runners as they passed us.

That worked for us for a couple of weeks until the teacher found out what was happening. Our punishment was to run the course twice with him observing us from a vantage point, so we ended up more tired than the others after running more miles than the others. We learned from our experience to do what was asked of us and I had to put up with long-distance running, whilst I remained at that school.

To some extent, my actions are paralleled to those of Jonah who also had lessons to learn and in his case, not from a P.E. teacher, but from a God whom he was called to obey.

We are not told much about Jonah's background, except that his father was called Amittai, and he was a Hebrew of sincere faith (Jonah 1:1, v9) from Gath Hepher near Nazareth in Zebulun, (2 Kings 14:25). His name means dove as is used in Hosea (Hosea 7:11). He is one of the 12 minor prophets of the Nevi'im (*The prophets*). The book is set in the reign of Jeroboam II (786–746 BC), King of the Northern Kingdom of Israel about 50 years before the Exile.

Jeroboam was an evil but successful king, according to Pastor Chuck Swindoll (b1934), an evangelist and writer in Texas, who reports: 'Israel's borders expand to their greatest extent since the time of Solomon. Increased prosperity resulted in a materialistic culture that thrived on injustice to the poor and oppressed.'

(*This was also*) one of the key messages of Jonah's prophetic contemporary, Amos'[85] (*Insertion mine*). Another contemporary around the same time as Jonah and Amos is Hosea who brings a similar message to Israel.

Bible Study Tools Christian support group points out that 'Unlike most other prophetic parts of the OT, this book is a narrative account of a single prophetic mission.'[86] The story unfolds in a mere 40 verses full of action, plus eight more verses in Jonah's poetic prayer.

Jonah is the central figure of the book and God commands him to go East to Nineveh,[87] the Assyrian capital city of more than 120,000 people, Israel's greatest enemy at the time. He is told to preach against the wickedness there and to warn the people of the imminent danger of divine judgment. He is therefore unusual in the OT in prophesying only to a Gentile nation.

Britannica informs, 'Jonah, like the Jews of the day, abhors even the idea of salvation for the Gentiles. God chastises him for his attitude, and the book affirms that God's mercy extends even to the inhabitants of a hated foreign city.'[88]

However, Jonah attempts to disobey God and travels West to Joppa, (modern *Jaffa*) on the coast and boards a boat for Tarshish (Jonah 1:3), in present-day Spain. This was as far West as he could reasonably travel, to the edge of the known world, in the Western Mediterranean.

Whilst on the boat, a huge and unexpected storm arose, sent by God (v4), and the sailors, who were probably God-fearing Jews (v16), realised this was no ordinary storm but had a connection with someone on board the ship, discovered by lottery that Jonah was to blame.

They linked Jonah's presence with his disobedience to God, 'The LORD, the God of heaven, who made the sea and the dry land…(*and it*) terrified them' (v9–10a) (*Insertion mine*).

When found out and awoken from his deep sleep, Jonah confirmed he was running away from God and felt so ashamed to be the cause of the storm he asked the sailors to throw him overboard. He was prepared to risk his own life in order to save the sailors. This was done and the storm calmed, so the sailors offered sacrifices to the LORD God.

As part of God's plan, Jonah doesn't die in the turbulent waters but is miraculously saved by a huge fish[89] provided by God to swallow him; this causes the raging storm to immediately become calm. God needed to get Jonah's attention and teach him a lesson in obedience.

Whilst in the fish's stomach with all the food it had swallowed recently, and in complete darkness, Jonah survives the swallowing and prays earnestly and sincerely with thankfulness to God for his mercy and promising to serve him as he requested.

He recognises his only means of escape is God and says as with our key verse, **'Salvation comes from the LORD'** (Jonah 2:9C).

GOD sees Jonah's humility and change of heart and commands the fish to vomit Jonah out onto dry land.

God, then, re-commissions Jonah again to travel to Nineveh and preach to the people there. This time, Jonah obeys God and walks for a day from the outskirts towards the city centre and warns the people by his preaching, 'Forty more days and Nineveh will be overthrown' (Jonah 3:4).

This cuts them to the heart; faith, fasting and repentance ensue. The endangered Ninevites, led by their king[90] appeal to God for mercy: people show their sorrow for sin by wearing sackcloth and ashes and cause even their animals to do the same. God sees this genuine remorse, forgives them and spares the city.

Wikipedia then concludes a summary of the result of this mass conversion:

'Displeased by this, Jonah refers to his earlier flight to Tarshish whilst asserting that since God is merciful, it was inevitable that God would turn from the threatened calamities. He then leaves the city and makes himself a shelter, waiting to see whether or not the city will be destroyed.'

'God causes a plant (in Hebrew a *kikayon*) to grow over Jonah's shelter to give him some shade from the sun. Later, God causes a worm to bite the plant's root and it withers. Jonah, now being exposed to the full force of the sun, becomes faint and pleads for God to kill him.'[91]

Jesus used the account of Jonah to answer the Pharisees and lawyers who wanted proof of who he was, so Jesus tells prophetically the parallel of him being dead for three days in the same way as Jonah was restricted in the fish for three days. He also said the positive response of the Ninevites shamed the Jews who were unwilling to repent, (Matthew 12:38–42 and Luke 11:29–30, v32).

Jesus said that as Jonah was three days in the fish's stomach so he would be three days in the heart of the Earth. He later repeats his use of the Jonah account this time to the Pharisees and Sadducees together, 'A wicked and adulterous generation looks for a sign, but none will be given it except the sign of Jonah' (Matthew 16:4).

Final thoughts

[1] The book of Jonah recounts real events in the life and ministry of a real person; a prophet with a clearly defined mission. In a sense, as with me and the cross-country running, he had instructions, failed to keep them, was found out, and sent a second time. God in his grace didn't punish Jonah for disobedience, as my P.E. teacher punished me! God commanded the fish to release Jonah (Jonah 2:10), before calling him to the task a second time (Jonah 3:1).

[2] We must note, the fish swallowed up Jonah, not to devour him, but to protect him. This fish was prepared by God and lay close to the ship ready to catch Jonah when he was thrown overboard, that he might keep Jonah from sinking to the bottom, and save him alive, though he was prepared to die because he had let God down (Jonah 1:12, v15, 2:4a).

[3] Matthew Henry (1662–1714), nonconformist minister and author, commented in 1706 on Jonah 1:17 that, 'Jonah was alive and well in the belly of the fish three days and three nights, not consumed by the heat of the animal, nor suffocated for want of air.'[92] His survival in that setting is itself a miracle.

[4] Jonah makes three amazing statements indicating his mature spiritual position:

-'I worship the LORD, the God of heaven' (Jonah 1:9).

-'Salvation comes from the LORD' (Jonah 2:9).

-'I knew that you are a gracious and compassionate God' (Jonah 4:2).

[5] Jesus identifies with Jonah's three days in the fish which foreshadows his three days 'in the heart of the earth' (Matthew 12:40b), before his resurrection. Conversely, Jonah by faith may well have had an insight into the actions of the Messiah to come hundreds of years later, that 'salvation comes from the LORD,' (Jonah 2:9), and that 'God is merciful' (Jonah 4:11).

[6] Jonah realised he was working against God at first and had to learn obedience coupled with a willing heart to do what God asks. Eventually, he left Israel for Assyria to take God's message but he was not happy at the outcome.

'To Jonah, this (*repentance and mass conversion of an enemy Gentile nation*) seemed very wrong, and he became angry' (Jonah 4:1) (*Insertion mine*).

The book concludes with God asserting his right to show 'concern' (Jonah 4:11) and as he said to Moses, 'I will have compassion on whom I will have compassion' (Exodus 33:19b).

[7] The sheer size of the population of Nineveh and the fact that they turned to God in repentance and faith, shows the grace and mercy of God (Jonah 3:10 and 4:11).

God is unchanging and 'The same yesterday and today and forever' (Hebrews 13:8); he can work the same miracles when he chooses to.

Questions to consider:

1. Jonah was called by God to sole missionary service. Why did he run away?
2. Do you think God provided a big fish to swallow Jonah?
3. What was the sign of Jonah Jesus spoke of in Matthew 16:4?

Gospel Days

9 Jesus and the Widow of Nain's Son

'When the Lord saw her, his heart went out to her and he said, "Don't cry"' (Luke 7:13).
Full story: (Luke 7:11–17)

One day, when I was in Africa, working for a charity, I went to a meeting on the equator high in the hills around Kisumu, the third largest city in Kenya. I went to meet a young man who was starting life after school as a carpenter. I was involved in giving him a grant to start his chosen profession and went to see how he was getting on and asked if I could help further. I was delighted with what I found.

He was working hard at quite a high altitude where it was not too hot, making furniture to a high standard and fulfilling commissions. He used most of the money from each commission to finance the timber for the next one and the work and a profit were coming in. He felt secure and had a big smile. He said he felt so blessed because so many of his friends didn't have a job. (I later checked the statistics and found that 33% of the young people under 25 were unemployed!)

Suddenly, a long way down the hill, about half a mile away, I saw a procession of people of all ages dressed in bright clothes singing and swaying to their music, full of life and joy and some played tambourines or other hand-held instruments. I asked my carpenter friend what was happening. He told me it was a funeral procession.

I asked why there was all the happiness and singing, and he told me it was a funeral of a Christian and so all the people of the village came together and were celebrating. The column of people was slowly winding their way through the fields and past scattered individual homes to the graveyard. There was no pressure on time, he said, and it would probably fill the whole day.

This made me think of too many funerals I have attended in England where everyone who could wear black and behaved in a polite way towards people they hadn't seen, sometimes for years. Some would travel quite a distance to be there. I thought of black limousines, the official funeral flowers and the numbers attending which were often low.

I have rarely seen joy or heard music at a funeral beyond the inclusion of one or two hymns. If it was a cremation, there was pressure to keep to the allocated time and then move out for the next cremation party to come into the crematorium chapel.

The contrast is obvious. Both styles have their place. But my experience from my numerous visits to the part of Africa I visited is that faith has clear roots in society and is expressed at every possible opportunity with joy.

As the Apostle Peter wrote, 'You believe in him and are filled with an inexpressible and glorious joy' (1 Peter 1:8b).

There can be joy on Earth and there is joy in heaven when a sinner turns to Christ for salvation (Luke 15:7).

It is good to have joy in worship and upon the passing on of a Christian from Earth to heaven in a funeral celebration (2 Corinthians 5:8).

Jesus was busy ministering in Capernaum, where there was a strong Roman military presence. He was preaching, teaching and healing. Jesus had been teaching that God's reign is one in which the poor receive the Kingdom of God (Luke 6:20), and weeping is turned to laughing (v21), then almost as if to prove his point, he healed the Roman centurion's servant (Luke 7:10).

Jesus may well have stayed in Capernaum that night and the next day, walked with his disciples, some women and a large crowd to Nain about 25 miles (40 km) away (Luke 8:1).[93]

In this town in a new location, the teaching was put into practice as the fame and popularity of Jesus continued to grow (Luke 7:11).

This was in the first year of Jesus' ministry so strong opposition to him had not yet developed. Luke, in his Gospel, relates the story which must have appealed to him as a doctor, as it involved someone being raised from the dead. He knew this was clinically impossible.[94] As Jesus approached the town gate he met a funeral procession (v12).

John Calvin (1509–1564), a French Protestant reformer adds that 'The dead man was carried out of the city in accordance with a very ancient custom among all nations.'[95]

The funeral is likely to have been in the style of funerals of the day: neither a noisy and joyful celebration nor a solemn and quietly dignified affair (as per my opening two examples). It would have been accompanied by lots of crying from a large number of townspeople who knew the widow and were with her in her grief. They considered this woman, who had lost her husband and is now facing a second death to be a tragedy.

At this town gate, the two contrasting crowds met.[96] It was probably awkward at first, as I have seen when lorry drivers going through a Cornish village where I lived to see a funeral moving from the church on the main road to the graveyard about 200 yards away. If travelling in the opposite direction, they slowed down and some doffed their caps very respectfully. That was the local custom.

Without a doubt, those joyfully arriving at Nain from Capernaum would have shown respect to those grieving on their way to the cemetery. Some in each group may have been uncomfortable, but one person was in complete control and he knew what he would do about this funeral procession. He was completely comfortable.

The woman in her grief wanted one thing: her son. She didn't reach out to Jesus. She didn't even show any faith. The woman says nothing and does nothing. Michael K. Marsh, priest in the Episcopal Church in the Diocese of West Texas informs us, 'Luke tells us nothing about her response to her son being raised from the dead and sitting up and talking.'

That is not because she has nothing to say but because Luke wants us to see and focus on something else. In some ways, the real miracle and the amazing thing about this story is the response of the crowds.'[97]

But Jesus saw the woman and immediately reached out to her with words of love, compassion and hope with our key words for this miracle where we read:

'When the LORD saw her, his heart went out to her and he said, "Don't cry"' (Luke 7:13).

Whilst the NIVUK has heart, KJV and others have *compassion*.

It was in compassion that the Good Samaritan acted, (Luke 10:33) (KJV), and the prodigal son's father acted in compassion towards his son (Luke 15:20).

Both of these parables and the Nain miracle are unique to Luke, and are not recorded by the other Gospels, suggesting Luke's observation of and high regard for compassion. Jesus has compassion for this woman. He understands her pain. She senses this in his words and hears it in his voice. He knows what she is going through better than anyone else, and he is there to help. In telling her not to cry he wants her to trust him.

He knows what he is doing and wants the woman to know that he is in control of the situation. He wants to comfort her with his words and actions. That is what he did (v13–14). The coffin bearers knew something important was happening so they stood still. Here was the unexpected.

Though some were being paid to cry, Jesus was saying to the woman, 'Don't cry.' In other words, don't be in despair.

It is also important to note the ability and willingness of Jesus to see the woman and that he is recorded a number of times in the Gospels as seeing those who are often invisible.

Any funeral is a loss to those left behind, and this was a huge loss. The dead boy was the only son of his widowed mother. The loss of her only son meant a miserable future for the widow who would now have no one to support her. In her culture, this was an economic disaster. She would not be able to work and earn as a woman and so she would be reduced to begging. That was the reality of her bleak future.

Jeremy Myers, pastor and writer, adds in his blog, 'Her immediate concern was that she had once again lost someone she loved dearly. Yes, nobody was going to provide for her, but worse, she was now alone. Completely alone. There is nobody for her to share her grief with.'[98]

She also had no prospect of any other children. In referring to Jesus, Luke uses the word LORD, which when used infrequently in the NT, indicates his Divinity. This is a very powerful message indeed. Luke is writing after the event and simply records what happened, and what was said.

In a sermon delivered at the Metropolitan Tabernacle, London, by C.H. Spurgeon (1834–1892), a Baptist minister, we read of the link between physical and spiritual death.

The sermon was entitled:

'Young Man, Is This for You? Luke 7:11–17.'[99]

Spurgeon says that:

'The spiritually dead, cause great grief to their gracious friends…For this grief, there is only one helper, but he can truly help.'

After calming the mother, Jesus then touched the bier or open coffin.[100] Without hesitation, Jesus then addresses the young man who rises from the dead and begins to talk (Luke 7:14). Jesus again addresses the mother (v15).

Matthew Henry comments on verse 15, 'When dead souls are raised to spiritual life, by divine power going with the Gospel, we must glorify God, and look upon it as a gracious visit to his people. Let us seek for such an interest in our compassionate Saviour, that we may look forward with joy to the time when the Redeemer's voice shall call forth all that are in their graves.'[101]

Matthew Poole (1624–1679), a nonconformist theologian, adds:

'Young man, I say unto thee, Arise; thereby declaring to them (would they have understood it) that he was the Son of God, and whilst he was on earth had power in and from himself by the word of his mouth to command the dead to arise. His word was effective, and to evidence it, it is said, that he that was dead sat up, so as all might take notice of the miracle, and began to speak.'

Luke records this in v14b and v15.[102] Many people in the two crowds were firstly afraid and then they thought about what they had witnessed and praised God for this miracle deciding that Jesus must be a prophet (v16), and spread the news far and wide throughout Judea and the whole region (v17).

Sarah Henrich, Professor of New Testament, Luther Seminary, Minnesota, tells us 'The people are in fear and excitement as they proclaim that:

"A great prophet has appeared among us" and "God has come to help his people" (Luke 7:16b). The crowd may not be fully cognisant of who Jesus is, but they are deeply correct.'[103]

Jesus spoke to the boy as if he were alive. The Apostle Paul explained this action to the church in Rome:

'God…gives life to the dead and calls into being things that were not' (Romans 4:17b).

The raising of the widow of Nain's son is one of three occasions when Jesus raised people from the dead. The other two are: Jairus's daughter (Luke 8:41–42, v49–56) and Lazarus (John 11:1–44).

Jesus came to bring real life (John 10:10), and overthrow the finality of death; it had to be defeated. At funerals recorded in the Gospels where Jesus attended, he raised the dead person to life. What a remarkable fact!

Final thoughts

[1] We have the barest details of the story but what we have is very challenging. Jesus said 10 words. Before the miracle one crowd was mourning, the other joyful. After the miracle, both crowds were filled with wonder and expressed their praise, declaring Jesus to be a *great prophet* and spreading the news about the miracle *throughout Judea and beyond* (Luke 7:16).

I would like to know what the mother said to Jesus or about the miracle, and what her son said since he was immediately talkative when he came back to life. One day when I get to heaven, I shall ask the widow and her son!

[2] We might like to consider why the LORD is moved to compassion by what he saw.

[3] Jesus was not prepared for death to have control of the situation, and he, as Sarah Hendrich says, 'Acts, not allowing even death to stop him.'[104]

[4] Luke begins his account with Jesus and a large, excited crowd who are in anticipation of what might happen next; he ends with an even larger crowd being his evangelists!

[5] For the woman tragedy turned into triumph; for the boy death turned into life.

We see how the crowd, the woman and the boy respond to this wonderful miracle. How does the story affect us the readers?

Questions to consider:

1. Should there be sadness or gladness at a funeral?
2. Why was the Widow of Nain and her son unnamed?
3. If you were the boy brought back to life, what would you say?

10 Jesus and the Woman at the Well

'Go, call your husband and come back' (John 4:16).

Full story: (John 4:4–30)

Living as I do in a Cornish village of about 100 people in a rural farming area I know many of the people. It's the sort of village where nearly everyone greets each other, and many give their predictions about what 'the weather will do' that day; the usual first topic of conversation. Twice a day I take our dog for a 20-minute walk. The walk, however, takes me about 40 minutes. The reason is that I meet some really interesting people and we chat for as long as it takes.

I plan to go home, as the Cornish say colloquially, *Dreckly*.[105] Some of these are dog walkers as well and the dogs pass on their news in their own way whilst waiting patiently for the owners to move on. It's also a chance for them to smell the smells and sit and watch the world go by, and wait for owners to *put the world right*!

I see people in their gardens, people going to the village shop, or visitors on holiday looking around with wonder and experiencing the peace and quiet of this beautiful area which is usually different from where they have come from.

When I get back home, my wife often says, 'Did you see anybody you know?'

I then relate who is ill and who is improving or recovering. Who has a new car or changed a barn on their land to holiday accommodation? I tell her of ladies I hear about who would appreciate a visit from my wife and tell her which farmers have now got the latest quarter of a million-pound tractor and which retired people now have electric cars.

If I can encourage someone or listen to someone, I will try and do so. Occasionally, the situation is right to share my Christian faith in conversation with a person prepared to listen.

This is similar to the situation in this miracle in which Jesus meets a really interesting person and shares his faith with her. It is, of course, different from my experience because she is in her home territory and Jesus is the visitor.

Jesus was ministering in Judea but the Pharisees were always on the lookout for things to criticise Jesus over, compared the number of baptisms of Jesus with John the Baptist. So, Jesus decided to withdraw from that district and not enter any discussion on the subject and return to Galilee.

As John the Apostle and Gospel writer tells us, 'Now, he had to go through Samaria' (John 4:4).[106]

And so the longest report and incident of the NT unfolds. Jesus is travelling from the South to the North and takes the most direct route but not one Jews would normally take. They would normally travel around Samaria and not through it.

This longer route is because the Jews 'regarded the Samaritans as foreigners and their attitude (*to them*) was often hostile, although they shared most beliefs, whilst many other Jews accepted Samaritans as either fellow Jews or as Samaritan Israelites. The two communities seemed to have drifted apart in the post-exilic period—' according to Wikipedia (*Insertion mine*).[107]

However, and in the conversation to come, this is a crucial point since the Samaritans regarded Mt Gerizim as the holy mountain and the Jews held onto Mt Zion (Jerusalem) as the focal point of their worship (John 4:20).[108]

The Gospel of John, as with Luke,[109] is favourable towards the Samaritans. Some of the final words of Jesus before his ascension include the Samaritans as he instructs his disciples, You will be my witnesses in Jerusalem, and in all Judea and Samaria, and to the ends of the earth (Act 1:8b).

In this story of the Woman at the Well, also called the Samaritan Woman, we see important themes of the Gospel. Jesus approached the unnamed woman and in doing so he demonstrated his care for everyone regardless of their background, gender or social standing by approaching her (John 4:7).

Her background would be very likely to cause her community to shun her. Later, at the end of the story, we can be impressed and inspired by her enthusiastic witnessing of the good news Jesus brought to her and to her people (v28–30, v42).

The woman lived at Sychar and Jesus was so tired from his walking and hot in the sun at its mid-day height, that he stopped at the well for a rest whilst the disciples went into town, about half a mile away, to buy food. The timing, as we saw in the previous chapter with the widow at Nain, was perfect.

The woman came out of town to fetch some water and Jesus asked her for a drink.

As Jews didn't associate with Samaritans, nor did men address women, it took her by surprise when Jesus made a request of her. If she had given him a drink, that would have made Jesus ritually unclean by accepting a drink from a Samaritan. The conversation then led to how she could ask him for a drink if she knew who he was. Her brittle tone indicates further her feeling of rejection.

She questioned him as to whether he was greater than Jacob,[110] who gave the well, the greatest Israelite she could think of in her background. Stephanie Englehart, author, and involved in a church plant in Seattle, concentrates on the woman's real need to be forgiveness and putting her life right with God.

She says, 'Jesus said his water would be totally satisfying so that a person who drinks it would not thirst again and it would give eternal life' (John 4:14).[111]

This really did appeal to the woman and she said it would also be good to be able to stop making the regular trip to the well (v15). She was beginning to realise that she was talking to someone very special and he was offering something very special, but she had much yet she needed to understand.

Jesus, then, changed direction and spoke to her about her personal life. He challenges the woman to be honest and face up to how she is living in the words:

'Go, call your husband and come back' (v16).

She admitted she didn't have a husband and Jesus filled in the gaps in her reply much to her amazement. He knew that she was ashamed of her lifestyle and needed love and forgiveness. He now had her full attention.

He probably said much more than John records, because she told her friends and neighbours that, 'Jesus told me everything I've ever done' (v39b).

The woman then switched direction to take attention from her personal life, of which she was not proud, to her community's worship at Mt Gerizim, and she knew the Jews held Mt Zion to be their centre of worship. Jesus then meets her challenge head-on and says God actually requires not worship at a place but sincere worship from the heart (v23). Jesus was making it quite clear that she didn't have to hide anything from God. She was accepted just as she was.

The woman then directs the conversation to the Samaritans looking for the Messiah to come, and here, she shows her personal belief, and says, 'When he comes, he will explain everything to us' (v25b).

'Then, Jesus declared, "I, the one speaking to you—I am he"' (v26).

The disciples returned and were shocked he was talking 'with a woman' (v27). They overlooked the fact she was also a Samaritan but they were afraid to ask Jesus why he was speaking to her, or what he wanted from her.

The woman not only recognised Jesus as a Jew, but she wondered if he was the Messiah (v27). She may well have realised that she was able to worship him in the spirit and in truth (v23), which is what God was looking for. In contrast, it took the disciples a long time for them to understand his Messiahship.

As Jessica Brodie, Christian novelist, journalist, editor, blogger, and writing coach explains, 'The woman, appeared to see through his parables and glimpse the truth behind his words when so many others, including Jewish experts and scholars, could not.'[112]

Meanwhile, the woman ran back into the town leaving her water jar behind to give her urgent news to the townspeople. This was the most important news she had ever encountered. She had been so challenged intellectually, emotionally and spiritually, that she impressed on those who knew her that the stranger revealed he knew lots of her secrets. And so, they quickly left the town to meet this stranger and see for themselves why she was so excited, and see if he was the Messiah (v30, v39).

In Sychar, this whole situation was unexpected and unimaginable, so when they heard the woman's report, the people were intrigued and went to find out for themselves what was happening and who the stranger was (v30). Ethnic and gender differences were ignored. The townspeople were so thrilled by what they discovered that they urged Jesus to stay with them and so for two days he stayed and taught them about salvation.

The National Shrine research group tell us, 'When Jesus walked the earth, Jews and Samaritans hated each other; in fact, many Jews would even cross the Jordan twice rather than pass through Samaria as Jesus did. Jews also did not eat or drink with Samaritans, who they viewed as lax in their standards of cleanliness.'[113]

It is interesting how in the unfolding of the conversation, the woman's perception of Jesus changed. First, she saw Jesus as a Jew (v9), then as a prophet (v19), then as the possible Messiah (v29). She knew there was something very special about Jesus. The woman's testimony was so vivid and believable that many came to personal faith even before they met him (v39). Once others had done so, even more, became believers (v41).

They said, 'We know that this man really is the Saviour of the world' (v42b).

Jack Zevada, reporter, editor, freelance writer and elder at a Lutheran Church in Missouri, points out the passage is important because Jesus, 'Cares for the outcasts of society. The Samaritan woman was considered inferior because of her sex, ethnicity, and relationship history, but none of that mattered to Jesus because he saw her need for salvation.'[114]

Jesus was proving he really was the Saviour of all people not just the Jews.

Avery Rimmiler, author and student in Transformational Entrepreneurship and Theology, notes:

'It was surprising, to find a woman there in the heat of the day. Usually, women would go together in groups to get water for their families and animals later in the day, when it was cooler. From this, we can guess that the woman at the well was an outcast, or even despised by the other women in town.'[115]

Just as the majority of Jews rejected Jesus as Messiah, so, in contrast, many Samaritans accepted him.

Luke tells us that Jesus told a Jew the expert in the law, to behave as the Good Samaritan did in that parable, and said, 'Go and do likewise' (Luke 10:37b).

Final thoughts

[1] There are a number of miracles in this story: Jesus breaking with convention and going through Samaria, the woman going alone to draw water, a male Jew addressing a female Samaritan, the woman being a persuasive missionary and fellow Samaritans becoming believers as a result, and so on.

But I believe the greatest miracle is that the woman is honest with Jesus about her circumstances and moves from wanting physical water to wanting spiritual water, and in doing so finds salvation: *the Messiah, the Saviour of the world* (John 4:29, v42).

[2] Jesus' conversation and actions were driven by his love for this woman and the other Samaritans. The Jews might have considered the Samaritans marginalised but the story shows that no one is beyond the limits of the love of Jesus. All people are equally important to him.

[3] This story, only recorded by John, as the longest in the Gospels, indicates its importance and why John chose to include it as one of a restricted number of miracles; in which John has his usual emphasis on theology and unveiling the true ministry of Jesus.

[4] The fact that Jesus stayed with the Samaritans for two days highlights the fact that Gentiles are important to Jesus and he will go out of his way to bring them into his kingdom.

[5] The encounter of Jesus and the Samaritan woman is not a random meeting. It was planned by God and depicts Jesus' mercy and love, especially as she has experienced rejection and disappointment.

[6] One short encounter with Jesus changed this woman's whole life and gave her the confidence to be a missionary with a message to tell.

[7] Despite moral weakness, background, gender and non-Jewish heritage, God's love and acceptance of the woman shines through. Jesus met the woman, and can meet anyone whose life is in a mess and bring healing to the past and spiritual life in abundance (John 10:10).

Avery Rimmiler sees God at work, and she says:

'Through his Holy Spirit, he will pour out the living water into our hearts, his goodness overflowing in us with his promises. His promise to the Jews was to bring salvation, and he extended that to the Samaritan woman and to us as well.'[116]

Questions to consider:

1. How did Jesus know about the Samaritan woman's background?
2. Are Gentiles equal to Jews? (Imagine the Samaritans were Gentiles for this consideration.)
3. What is the spiritual water Jesus was speaking of in John 4:29 and v42?

Victory Days

11 Jesus and Palm Sunday

'What are you doing, untying that colt?' (Mark 11:5b)

Full story: (Mark 11:1–11)

I try and imagine what it would look like if, in my village, I saw the keys in a car's ignition, got into it and drove it away in front of the owner leaning on his garden fence. Or if I saw a neighbour going out to the village shop and I was seen going into their empty house to make a cup of tea because I knew the front door was unlocked.

It is this sort of situation which happened on one particular day, probably the day after the Sabbath, when Jesus despatched two of his disciples to bring to him a donkey at Bethphage by the Mount of Olives. The reason for needing the donkey for a short journey would soon become clear, but Jesus didn't tell his disciples to get permission first.

The story recorded by the Gospels we now celebrate and call Palm Sunday. This, as Wikipedia informs, 'Commemorates Jesus Triumphal Entry into Jerusalem; an event mentioned in each of the four canonical Gospels. Palm Sunday marks the first day of Holy Week.'[117] (Matthew 21:1–11, Mark 11:1–11, Luke 19:28–44 and John 12:12–19).

Jesus told his disciples to find the colt and bring it to him with its mother (Matthew 21:2).

The colt had never been ridden before. It was an unusual thing to do to ride on a donkey's colt, rather than ride on a horse or in a chariot, and this sent a message to the crowd: that of humility. This riding into Jerusalem was an act the Jews would recognise as an impending coronation and in this Jesus is alluding to being king of his own kingdom.

He was entering the city of David and it was customary for a king about to be crowned to enter the city riding on an animal to show the importance of the event.[118]

Jesus did come as a king, but was a spiritual king of peace and not an earthly king victorious in war or ready for war. Horses were majestic animals and often the choice mount of a king symbolic of majesty and power: they were beasts of war. When a king rode out to meet his enemy in battle, he would do so on a horse. The Jews were hoping for a conquering king, one who would end the Roman occupation and establish Israel with its own independent rule.

Jesus' choice of a donkey gave a different message. It was an animal that signified peace. He did not come to wage war against Rome as the people hoped, but to bring peace to individual people. This peace, proclaimed by angels at his birth (Luke 2:14), was not between hostile nations, but between sinful people and God.

Jesus knew that the taking of the animals would be challenged by the owners, so he told the disciples what to say when questioned. Here we get our key words for this miracle:

'What are you doing, untying that colt?' (Mark 11:5b)

The story shows that the owner or owners knew who Jesus was and knew him as *LORD* (Matthew 21:3, Mark 11:3 and Luke 19:34). He was not just a person with a position such as Rabbi, or Pharisee, or a person by name or job, such as carpenter from Galilee, and it suggests that the owner may well have been a devout believer and even part of the wider group around Jesus. Mark tells us cloaks were thrown over the donkey for a saddle and some threw palm branches on the road.

The crowds took up the chant of *Hosanna*, meaning *save*, as part of their jubilant praise and celebration. They were heralding the coming of a king, and in their minds, wanted him to save them from the despised Romans. For Jesus, this act had a far deeper significance which was beyond most onlookers to understand.

It was this record of the Triumphal Entry into Jerusalem which prompted Theodulf, Bishop of Orleans, an Italian living in France (750–821 AD) to write the well-known hymn, *All glory laud and honour*, and include it in the second verse:

'The people of the Hebrews,
With palms before thee went,
Our praise and prayer and anthems,
Before thee we present.'[119]

John makes it clear that the disciples understood the passion story only after the resurrection when they then saw it as the fulfilment of prophecy, 'At first his disciples did not understand all this. Only after Jesus was glorified did they realise that these things had been written about him and that these things had been done to him' (John 12:16).

All of this unbridled celebration disturbed the Pharisees because they saw that the ordinary people were in awe of Jesus who had just raised Lazarus from the dead, and the city was buzzing about it. Jesus was popular and had an increasingly large following. Thus, the Pharisees were constantly looking for ways of stopping him from healing and teaching which made him so admired.

But that made them so jealous and angry and showed them to be so insignificant in comparison. The Pharisees would have understood the importance of Jesus' actions in behaving like a king about to be crowned, but they refused to see the spiritual meaning. The crowds greeting him entering Jerusalem in this spectacular way were, therefore, too much for them to accept.

Jesus had a great following and they didn't, so almost in despair and discouraged as his fame rose, and their efforts proved to be so ineffective that they said to one another, 'See, this is getting us nowhere. Look how the whole world has gone after him!' (John 12:19)

The actions of Jesus were linked by Matthew to prophecy and Messianic promises specifically for the benefit of his Jewish audience, (Matthew 21:4, v10–11).

He alone mentions that Jesus enters Jerusalem with the donkey and colt, (the other Gospel writers mention one animal), as foretold by Zechariah, 'Rejoice greatly, Daughter Zion! Shout, Daughter Jerusalem! See, your king comes to you, righteous and victorious, lowly and riding on a donkey, on a colt, the foal of a donkey' (Zechariah 9:9).[120]

The Gospels show how the presence of Jesus calms many situations, including this one where the young colt shows no unease.

Donkeys in the OT are generally linked with work in the fields, 'The oxen and donkeys that work the soil will eat fodder and mash, spread out with fork and shovel' (Isaiah 30:24).

They are animals at work in peaceful times when the land was farmed.[121] This is in contrast to times of war. When the Promised Land was threatened, the men would leave their fields, take up arms and fight their enemies. If they had them available, horses would be used. Stephen Baker, contributing author with Salem Web Network, Ohio, writes:

'Jesus rode a donkey in part to protest against the Jews, telling them he would not be the military king that they desired.'[122]

Many people failed to see in Jesus that he was the Messiah. On a number of occasions, the ordinary people wanted to make him king by force (John 6:15), and Pilate wanted to free him at his trial referring to him as king of the Jews (John 19:10, v14).

Yet, they shouted out as he was carried by the donkey into Jerusalem, *Hosanna* (John 12:13) save (us)!

A few days later, as these same supporters turned against him shouting for him to be crucified, Jesus said from the cross on Good

Friday, 'Father, forgive them, they do not know what they are doing' (Luke 23:34).

Neither did most of them know what they were saying on the Sunday we call Palm Sunday!

There are miraculous elements to this story, and these are revealed in Mark's account. It is likely that he got most of his eyewitness material for his book: his Gospel which bears his name, from Peter his friend and one of Jesus' inner group of three with James and John.[123] Peter was greatly touched by the last week in the life on Earth of Jesus.

This Passion Week had a triumphal event at the beginning and end: Palm Sunday and Easter Sunday. This week was so important to Peter and hence to Mark, that it occupies a third of his book, and he ignores the birth story of Jesus as found in the other Gospels. The birth story was, as is clear in Mark's omission of it, was to him much less important than Passion Week.

Central to this Triumphal Entry is the request from Jesus in which he simply names himself as *the LORD* (Mark 11:2), and this deserves attention. This is both an intimate title and shows a developed and sincere personal faith on the part of the donkey owners who knew Jesus as *the LORD*.

They must have had a committed faith because they didn't question why the donkeys were being taken away and knew from the disciples' answer to their question who had made the request.

Others, such as the man born blind when questioned by the Pharisees as to who gave him his sight, said all that he knew was that it was, 'The man they call Jesus—' (John 9:11a).

In the Garden of Gethsemane at his arrest, the 'Soldiers and some officials from the chief priests and the Pharisees, said they were looking for Jesus of Nazareth—' (John 18:3, v5a).

There is no mention of Jesus being their LORD on those occasions.

One of Jesus' closest friends was the disciple, Judas. At the Passover meal, we call the Last Supper, Jesus passed the bread to Judas. 'As soon as Judas took the bread, Satan entered into him' (John 13:27).

He knew Jesus was the Christ, the anointed one but never really knew him. He betrayed Jesus and as such was branded by John in writing his Gospel, 'the traitor' (John 18:5).

Once Jesus was tried and condemned, 'Judas was seized with remorse…and hanged himself' (Matthew 27:3, v5).

Judas certainly didn't know Jesus as his LORD.

After the resurrection, 10 of the remaining 11 disciples saw the risen Jesus. 'But Thomas…was not with the disciples when Jesus came. So the other disciples told him, "We have seen the LORD!"'

But Thomas didn't believe them until Jesus came into a locked room where this time Thomas was with the others and, 'Jesus came and stood among them Thomas said to him, "My LORD and my God!"' (John 20:26, v28).

All 11 disciples, now, seemed to know Jesus as LORD. We are told, 'No one can say, "Jesus is LORD", except by the Holy Spirit.' (1 Corinthians 12:3b).[124]

So, what are we seeing here? Firstly, we have Jewish traditions and history which provide the story's background and foundation and so set the scene for the Triumphal Entry. Secondly, we have some very interesting details of this day as reported in Mark 11.

Final thoughts

[1] Two disciples obeyed without question the command of Jesus to find and take the donkey and its colt without asking permission (Mark 11:4).

[2] The colt was tied up (v4) and had never experienced being ridden (v2).

[3] Jesus knew in advance that the action would be challenged and so he gave the disciples the words of explanation naming himself as *the LORD* to give authority. He knew that the owners of the donkeys would know to whom that referred. He did not need to introduce himself as Master, Rabbi or by name (v3).

[4] We see that Jesus had also told his two disciples that he would return the donkeys after use (v3). He gave attention to every detail.

[5] The donkey owners allowed the donkeys to go (v6) when they were told the Lord needed them and would return them. They knew and trusted Jesus, even though he didn't tell either the disciples or the donkey owners why he wanted the donkeys. On the naming of the title of Jesus, they released the donkeys without further questions.

[6] People naturally spread out their cloaks on the road and made a saddle for Jesus to sit on. Other people went to the fields and cut down palm branches to wave (v7–8). This was their custom at the Feast of Tabernacles (Leviticus 23:40), and as a sign which heralded the coming of the Messianic king and kingdom (John 12:12–13).[125]

[7] The crowds knew and used the words of the Messianic prophecy (Mark 11:9–10) where the king would ride into Jerusalem (Zechariah 9:9). So, they welcomed Jesus as a king like David. And together with pilgrims, there for the festival were welcoming what they thought was a possible overthrow of the physical kingdom of the Roman occupation.

[8] In Jerusalem, Jesus went to the temple which was on the extensive Temple Mount and occupied a quarter of Jerusalem. This was the physical centre of the Jewish kingdom of Israel and of their religious worship and the focal point of the coming Passover festival a few days later.

After surveying life and behaviour in the temple (Mark 11:11), Jesus took the disciples to rest in Bethany about two miles away where it was important to arrive before dark to secure accommodation. No doubt they would be tired after an exhausting and unexpectedly eventful day. As ever, with further attention to detail, Jesus knew and met their needs.

[9] A very obvious and important feature of this story, and the reason I have included Palm Sunday and the Colt; The Triumphal Entry, as a miracle in my selection of miracles, is because of the way the donkey owners released the donkeys to Jesus (v6) following the briefest conversation.

The Jewish history and traditions, the time of Passover and key people knowing Jesus as LORD, made this release of the donkeys a remarkable miracle.

Questions to consider:

1. On Palm Sunday why did Jesus choose a donkey rather than a horse to enter Jerusalem?
2. What made the crowds change from praising to hating Jesus?
3. What is the difference between Jesus as Saviour and Jesus as Lord in Mark 11:3?

12 Jesus: The Crucifixion and the Resurrection

'**And when Jesus had cried out again in a loud voice, he gave up his spirit**' (Matthew 27:50).
'**The angel said, "He is not here; he has risen, just as he said. Come and see the place where he lay"**' (Matthew 28:5–6).
Full story: (Matthew 27:32–28:15, Mark 15:21–16:18, Luke 23:26–24:49 and John 19:16 21:14)

A couple of years ago, I listened to some interviews on BBC radio and heard a man who was really frustrated with life because of its complexity and clutter. His home and his life seemed to have so much packed into it which held very little value to him so he decided to de-clutter and start again.

He kept his home and furniture and had only 100 personal possessions. I'm not sure if he was married or had a partner. But I imagine, it would not go down well if his wife or partner was unsympathetic!

He counted his chosen possessions and got rid of the rest. Shoes counted as one and he had a watch, radio, a knife, a fork and spoon, and so on. He had a book, a shirt, a towel, a holdall (ten things so far), and onwards to 100 items.

I think that approach would have frustrated me, although I can identify with how we are with possessions, or stuff and very soon if it were me I would quickly be up to 100 and life would be very stark. The last I heard this man continued his simple approach to life.

Another man who was interviewed admitted he was also finding life too cluttered, so he decided to live for a year with a herd of goats in the open air. He decided to eat and drink what the goats had and sleep alongside them and abandon his home, but he kept it for after the year when he planned to re-occupy it. The first day he felt completely happy and liberated.

The night wasn't so good because he didn't sleep so well. There were noises which kept him awake, he was cold, and the ground was more wet in the morning with dew than he expected. However, he thought as time passed it would get easier. But he was wrong.

He lasted three days, then hungry and tired, returned to his own home deciding that it was all right for goats to live outdoors and eat grass, nettles and weeds but not for him.

Both are examples of men trying to devise a plan and, in their case, implement the plan. (I notice there are no women trying these experiments!) I don't envy either of the men. I like my home comforts too much and living with my wife, and having relatives, friends and neighbours nearby.

We are told that God created people on Earth, but before that, he had a plan. This was to live with them as one of them and yet as God. He knew what would happen as a result of giving people free will. He knew people would fail and fall away from him, so his plan included making it possible to return to a relationship with him by faith through grace (Ephesians 2:8–9).

This was not an experiment but a pre-ordained plan even before he created the world. He chose to have a family, a kingdom, and a worshipping community with him in heaven. This required his gift of salvation, the giving of his own life, and the receiving of eternal life by those who accepted him. This was the predestined plan.

In the following Bible verses, we find God, as a Trinity of Father, Son and Holy Spirit, has always existed, and before ever the world was created he knew individuals who would respond to his love and be saved by grace through faith. They were chosen before the world and time began.

-God is '(*The*) high and lofty One that inhabiteth eternity' (Isaiah 57:15 KJV).

-God says wisdom (*infinite and eternal truth*) 'Was formed long ages ago, at the very beginning, when the world came to be' (Proverbs 8:23).

-God says of Jesus that 'He was chosen before the creation of the world' (1 Peter 1:20).

-God the Holy Spirit 'Was hovering over the waters (*of the created earth*)' (Genesis 1:2).

-God says we were chosen in 'Christ Jesus before the beginning of time' (2 Timothy 1:9).

-God says we are elect and 'In the hope of eternal life, which God, who does not lie, promised before the beginning of time' (Titus 1:2) (Romans 6:23)

(*parentheses in the texts mine*).

This is why we are now looking at the greatest miracle in the Bible, and I believe in the whole of human history; that God should come to Earth in the person of the LORD Jesus Christ.

'He came to seek and to save the lost' (Luke 19:10b).

He came to seek by being born and living as a human being; he came to save the lost by dying a cruel death on a cross. What a miracle that he came alive again after three days and lives forever in his kingdom in heaven and in the hearts of those who love him!

We must, therefore, examine the crucifixion and resurrection and see the facts in order to make up our own minds about how they affect us and decide how we should respond.

Easter is the high point, the focal point of the Christian faith when these amazing events happened. It embodies sacrifice, forgiveness and new life at the heart of the Christian Gospel message.

History, particularly that of the Jews, embodied in over 300 prophesies, pointing to Jesus, led to this one event with particular things happening on particular days in one momentous week. The following details are mostly taken from Luke's Gospel.

Triumphal Entry

A week before Easter Sunday on Palm Sunday there was the Triumphal Entry into Jerusalem (Luke 19:35–38).

As our miracle of the donkey colt carrying Jesus, and her mother alongside showed us, crowds of excited residents and pilgrims greeted him, waving palm branches and shouting out unashamedly, 'Blessed is the king who comes in the name of the LORD! Peace in heaven and glory in the highest!' (v38)

Many in the crowds, including his own disciples were looking for a conquering warrior king to free them from Rome, but they eventually had to learn that the kingdom of Jesus was a spiritual kingdom.

'Jesus said, "My kingdom is not of this world"' (John 18:36a), and was not achieved by force but by faith.

Teaching

During the weekdays of Monday to Thursday, Jesus was teaching the disciples and the crowds who came to hear him, about the Kingdom of God (Luke 21:37–38).

He answered criticism of his authority and taught meaningful parables. He also warned the disciples of turmoil to come such as the temple being destroyed, 'As for what you see here, the time will come when not one stone will be left on another; every one of them will be thrown down' (Luke 21:6).

Some listened in to these warnings to his disciples. These and similar words from Jesus were used at his trial against him (Matthew 26:62), when those judging him searched for accusations which would hold, as opposed to those whose testimonies were rejected as baseless.

Last Supper

Jesus organised the Passover meal for his disciples held on the Thursday evening. This was an annual reminder for the Jews of the departure of their ancestors from slavery in Egypt and of the way they left.[126] He explained how the meal was also to be celebrated in the future as a reminder of him and his sacrifice when the coming events had unfolded and they understood the significance.

He said, 'This is my body given for you; do this in remembrance of me' (Luke 22:19b).

This indicated that people could be freed from spiritual slavery. At the time, the disciples didn't realise what was coming and what he meant.[127]

Gethsemane

The garden of Gethsemane, at the foot of the Mount of Olives (Matthew 26:36), is a grove of olive trees that is still there in Jerusalem.

Specialists have calculated that some of the trees are over 2,000 years old and, therefore, would have been young trees at the time Jesus was there on the night he was arrested. As Jesus prayed in the garden, with some of his disciples: Peter, James and John whom he expected to watch him, he would have a view of the temple on the Temple Mount.

He would have been very aware of people gathering for the Passover. It is here that he prayed the most agonising prayer knowing what was to come. It would be here where he predicted Peter's denial and prayed for God's will to be done, saying, 'Father, if you are willing, take this cup from me; yet not my will, but yours be done' (Luke 22:42).

Trial

Jesus went through several sham trials, and according to Jason Saroski, a writer and Pastor of Calvary Longmont Church, Colorado, 'All of them were legally out-of-line, even by ancient standards. His first trial was before the Sanhedrin, the leading council of Israel, where he was charged with blasphemy for claiming to be God. The meeting of the council was called at night, and all the witnesses brought against Jesus were poor witnesses at best.'[128]

The chief priests, Sanhedrin and others tried him and eventually found him to be guilty of threatening to destroy the temple and of blasphemy (Mark 14:58, 64a) and returned him to Pilate to carry out their wishes to have him killed since they considered he was *worthy of death* (Matthew 26:66).

Pilate finally allowed his crucifixion in order to *satisfy the crowd* (Mark 15:15).

Crucifixion

On the following day, we call Good Friday, the crucifixion took place.[129] The death of Jesus was not that of any ordinary man. He could not even be described as just a good man. He was God dying to establish his kingdom in triumph over the kingdom of Satan on Earth. It was a day of victory and not of failure. About 27 years later in 57 AD, the Apostle Paul considered it a crucial day.

To the Christians at Corinth, he wrote, 'For what I received I passed on to you (*is*) of first importance: that Christ died for our sins according to the Scriptures, that he was buried, that he was raised on the third day according to the Scriptures' (1 Corinthians 15:3–4) (*insertion mine*).

On this day, Jesus was tortured, suffered and died for the sins of all people for all time. Sin is the reason for the death of Jesus, not the Roman authorities, not the Jewish leaders, nor the people who were whipped into a frenzy and shouted for it to happen—though all these had a measure of guilt.

Isaiah prophesied that this would happen some 700 years earlier:

'We all, like sheep have gone astray, each of us has turned to our own way and the LORD has laid on him the iniquity of us all' (Isaiah 53:6).

No one took the life of Jesus by force, he gave his life freely.

Jesus was crucified on a hill known as *The Skull* outside of Jerusalem.[130] As Jesus died, there was an eclipse, and the curtain of the temple was torn in two from top to bottom. The repentant thief asked to be remembered when Jesus came into his kingdom (Luke 23:42), and Jesus gave him that reassurance.[131]

Then, we read some of our key words for this miracle:

'And when Jesus had cried out again in a loud voice, he gave up his spirit' (Matthew 27:50).

Death

When Jesus died, his followers were devastated. The one whom they followed and believed in had died the death of a common criminal, alongside two thieves. Besides the eclipse and the torn curtain, Matthew gives us other details, mostly unique to his Gospel:

'The earth shook, the rocks split and the tombs broke open. The bodies of many holy people who had died were raised to life. They came out of the tombs after Jesus' resurrection, went into the holy city and appeared to many people. When the centurion and those with him who were guarding Jesus saw the earthquake and all that had happened, they were terrified, and exclaimed, "Surely he was the Son of God!"' (Matthew 27:51–54)

The bodies of godly people were raised and presumably stayed in the area of the tombs until Jesus was raised from the dead. The centurion and his detachment of soldiers saw the physical reaction in the sky, in the temple and on the ground and were watching the dignity of Jesus and heard his words; they knew Jesus had truly died.

Their conclusion was that he was the Son of God. This is a wonderful conclusion to reach by professional soldiers who had conducted many crucifixions.

Burial

After the crucifixion, a man named Joseph from Arimathea asked for the body of Jesus to be placed in his own private tomb (John 19:41). Joseph was a wealthy man, a member of the Sanhedrin, the national ruling council, and a follower of Jesus, as was Nicodemus another believer (Luke 23:50–51 and John 19:39) who helped him.

After they had hastily prepared his body for burial, because of the coming Sabbath at sundown, a large stone was rolled in front of the entrance, and Roman guards were placed in front of it (Matthew 27:64). It was sealed with a special seal that no one would dare to open.

Resurrection

Early on Sunday morning, once the Sabbath was completed at sunrise (Matthew 28:1) the tomb was found by Mary Magdalene to be empty.

Here, we read our other key words for this miracle:

'The angel said, "He is not here; he has risen, just as he said. Come and see the place where he lay"' (Matthew 28:5–6).

Robert Lowry, (1826–1899) an American professor of English literature, preacher and hymn writer, wrote the immortal words in 1874, 'Up from the grave he arose…Hallelujah! Christ arose!'[132]

Jesus met Mary in the garden and made a number of resurrection appearances. Paul reminded the Corinthians that Jesus, 'Appeared to Cephas (*Peter*), and then to the Twelve. After that, he appeared to more than five hundred of the brothers and sisters at the same time, most of whom are still living, though some have fallen asleep. Then, he appeared to James, then to all the apostles, and last of all he appeared to me' (1 Corinthians 15:5–8). (*Insertion mine*)

Because Jesus was raised, Paul wrote to Christians in Rome to say that we can also be raised, 'For if we have been united with him in a death like his, we will certainly also be united with him in a resurrection like his' (Romans 6:5).

It is hard to know exactly how the resurrection happened, but we and the witnesses at the time, both believers and many secular people, know that it did!

As ever, with his brilliant mind and grasp of medical facts and truth, Luke says of the women:

'They found the stone rolled away from the tomb, but when they entered, they did not find the body of the LORD Jesus' (Luke 24:2–3).

Response to the Resurrection

Early in his three-year ministry, Jesus had a conversation with Nicodemus, a Pharisee and member of the greater court of the Sanhedrin.

Jesus told him quite simply, 'Very truly, I tell you, no one can see the Kingdom of God unless they are born again' (John 3:3).

This conversation had a profound effect on Nicodemus who spoke up for Jesus with the Sanhedrin (John 7:50–51) and then helped Joseph of Arimathea with the burial of Jesus (John 19:39), as mentioned earlier.

It seems clear, even before the resurrection that Nicodemus together with Joseph of Arimathea, had come into the new birth. Now, after the resurrection, repentance towards God and faith in Jesus Christ as Saviour brings a person into new birth and the Kingdom of God, and so to receive eternal life.

Peter wrote, 'In his great mercy he has given us new birth into a living hope through the resurrection of Jesus Christ from the dead' (1 Peter 1:3).

If we truly believe he is who he says he is and that he rose from the dead as he said he would, and we know he is alive today, it will forever change the way we think and live.

Writing this chapter as I am at Easter, I find the details both fascinating and challenging. In Christian circles, people may say, *you must take up your cross* as a response to having difficulties in life. This doesn't compare with the actual very heavy cross that Jesus literally carried until he collapsed under its weight, having been severely flogged first, and Simon from Cyrene was forced to carry it for him (Luke 23:26).

All I had to do today was carry a two-metre-tall oak cross round the corner from my home to the church grounds and place it for onlookers to see for this weekend, but I found myself looking over my shoulder to see who might be looking at me. I tried hard not to be self-conscious. When I think of what Jesus went through for me, it was the very least I could do for him!

In the hymn, *The Old Rugged Cross* by George Bennard (1873–1958), a Methodist Evangelist in Ohio, written in 1912, the words of the chorus came to me with new force:

'So, I'll cherish the old rugged cross,
Till my trophies at last I lay down.
I will cling to the old rugged cross,
And exchange it for a crown.'[133]

I can say that this chapter and miracle have greatly touched me. It has not been easy to write. I remember again as a person with personal faith I must not be ashamed of Jesus my Saviour and LORD!

Final thoughts

[1] In the hymn, *There is a Green Hill Far Away* by Cecil Frances Alexander (1818–1895), a female Irish hymn writer and poet,[134] written in 1848, we read the words in verse 3:

'He died that we might be forgiven, he died to make us good. That we might go at last to heaven, Saved by his precious blood.'

This puts the death of Jesus in context and gives a simple explanation:

His *death* achieved much; it cancelled sin for the sinner.

His *resurrection* achieved much; it made eternal life possible for the sinner.

[2] As we consider the resurrection, we celebrate Jesus rising from the dead. I believe the resurrection happened, and because of it, this is the clearest proof that Jesus is exactly who he claimed to be—the Son of God and the only Saviour of the world.[135]

[3] Jesus made the ultimate sacrifice at the time of the annual Passover. He also had to be taken down from the cross before sunset on Friday, because this was the beginning of the Sabbath. These facts fit well into Judaism and its expectations and fulfil prophecy.

[4] When Jesus rose from the dead and walked out of the tomb, at that moment sin and death were defeated once and for always, for all people, for all time[136] and Jesus' kingdom was established![137]

[5] Bethany Jett, writer, author and conference speaker from Florida, concludes her timeline study:

'As we reflect on Jesus' time before the crucifixion, on the cross, and then the empty tomb on Sunday morning, let us remember that our God sacrificed his own Son so that we live eternally with him in heaven.'[138]

[6] The death and resurrection of Jesus brought about by God in his grace, assures us of the existence of the Godhead, and so there is hope for this hopeless world.

God in Jesus proved he understands us because he became like us but without sin. Jesus died for us, so we must live for him!

Questions to consider:

1. If you could have only 100 possessions, what would be in your top 10?
2. Who is God's elect in Titus 1:1?
3. Why did Jesus have to die? (Matthew 27:51–54)

Outreach Days

13 Peter and John

'He went…walking and jumping, and praising God' (Act 3:8).
Full story: (Act 3:1–10)

For a number of years, I worked in a large special school in an outer London borough. The pupils had complex physical and learning needs and our catchment area was quite wide because the school was well-resourced and had a very good reputation for successful educational provision. It was a good school providing quality teaching and learning.

However, I lived about 35 miles (56 km) away. I had to be up early in the morning and get into my journey by car before the commuter traffic built up on the M25 motorway and arterial roads going into London, and I arrived quite a while before the pupils to prepare for the day. Sometimes I felt very tired in the mornings and as I drove I felt I had various aches and pains.

The more I thought about it, the worse I felt, and occasionally, I felt discouraged. That was until the pupils arrived. They were so cheerful despite their huge personal challenges. Two-thirds were wheel-chair users and most had some type of brace—supporting arms, legs, head and so on.

About 10 relied on sophisticated electronic aids to speak for them and about 20 relied on eye pointing to indicate their needs. Nearly all the pupils in the school used Sign Supported Language to help them communicate or other non-verbal communication.

Looking at the pupils and interacting with them soon caused me to forget myself and how I felt. It was no longer relevant. Many times a day, I prayed for the children and staff and considered it a privilege to be working with them. Always I was thankful for all they taught me and I was humbled by how thankful they were for so many things they could achieve. Things, as simple as giving the Makaton[139] sign for *yes* and *no*!

One thing which excites me is that as with Peter and John, God in his grace and wisdom has given me a heart for those with disabilities. The miracle in this chapter concerns a man with a serious disability.

He met Jesus through the Holy Spirit's working through these two disciples who were simply going to the temple to pray. The outcome for him was life changing. This is the first healing miracle in the book of Acts.

The apostles and the first believers attended the temple worship at the usual times of prayer. Peter and John seem to have been led by God to bring healing to a man (unnamed as with so many special people in the Bible), disabled from birth, and a broken man at that, humiliated and in a hopeless condition. He had probably been carried to his regular place to beg for many years by friends, and was over 40 years old (Act 4:22).

He was totally dependent on the generosity of others for his survival. Peter, supported by John commanded him in the name of Jesus Christ of Nazareth to walk. This was the very thing he couldn't do!

Peter helped him to his feet and he jumped up and, **'He went...walking and jumping, and praising God'** (Act 3:8).

The details of this miracle are fully worthy of consideration.

What we have in Act 3 is a miracle in the first 10 verses followed by a sermon prompted by this incident in the following 15 verses, (Acts 3:11–26).

Here, we concentrate on the miracle. It gave Peter and John a perfect setting, having got the attention of many who were there at the time, and others who came running to join the crowd, for preaching the Gospel as an explanation of the miracle which they had witnessed.

Christianity, and the number of believers, was rapidly increasing. The Holy Spirit had come down on the Day of Pentecost and on that day alone 'Three thousand were added to their number—' (Act 2:41b).

However, on this occasion, a single person was the focus of attention, and at that moment, with his disability, he was more important than a religious meeting for prayer. To Peter and John, this man in his sad situation required justice and healing.

Amos, an OT prophet aimed for this and wrote:

'But let justice roll on like a river, righteousness like a never-failing stream!' (Amos 5:24)

The four pillars of discipline and belief of the Early Church were established: teaching, fellowship, breaking of bread and prayer (Act 2:42), and 'Everyone was filled with awe at the many wonders and signs performed by the apostles' (v43).

So, here at the healing of the disabled man was one of the *wonders and signs* which were happening amongst them.

As we see from the Gospels, Peter and John[140] were two of the three leading apostles, the other being James who became established as the leader of the Jerusalem church.

Peter and John, who were fishermen and partners together on the sea of Galilee before Jesus called them to join him, were often together and are thought to have been together in the high priest's palace at the trial of Jesus; because John knew the high priest, and because of that, he was able to get Peter inside the courtyard (John 18:15–16).

They ran together to Jesus' tomb. John was the faster runner (John 20:2–4).

They now went together to the temple. Peter and John in formal Jewish practice went regularly to the temple to pray together and continued as faithful Jews despite the exciting days after Pentecost Sunday.[141]

The CSB Study Bible points out, 'Peter and John continued to participate in Jewish rituals and worship, and early Christians regularly gathered in the temple. The full and final split of Christianity from Judaism came (*with*) the first Jewish revolt against Rome (AD 66–70) (*Insertion mine*).'[142]

'All the believers…every day continued to meet together in the temple courts' (Act 2:46).

The house of prayer and the hour of prayer (3 pm)[143] are both very important to them as faithful Jews (Act 3:1).

According to John Gill (1697–1771), whose commentary was published in 1763, a Baptist theologian, writer and minister, 'This was one of their hours of prayer; it was customary with the Jews to pray three times a day, not that these were times of divine appointment.'[144]

Gill says it may have been the Sunday after Pentecost. At this point, Peter and John did not abandon their Jewish faith.

The man who saw Peter and John passing was a poor, lame beggar with paralysis in his feet and ankles (v7) from birth.

He was unable to walk or work and was totally dependent on the compassion of others. Friends, for whom he must have been very thankful, laid him daily at one of the temple gates. He was visible but yet invisible to most of the people who passed by in this busy place. It was a beautiful and magnificent gate between the courts of the Jews and Gentiles and he probably only begged of Jews, so, he asked Peter and John for money.

According to Tony Merida, writer and founding Pastor of a church in North Carolina, 'There are three foundations of the Jewish faith: the Torah, worship, and showing kindness (giving alms).'

Since these activities were part of the rhythm of the religious community; individual beggars chose a visible location to ask for alms of people going up for prayer.[145]

Near this spot, Jesus rejected those making money (Matthew 21:12) but accepted, 'The blind and the lame (*who*) came to him at the temple, and he healed them' (v14) (*Insertion mine*).

With this particular man, Peter and John looked straight at him with compassion and a fixed gaze. This raised the man's attention and expectation. Peter then turned the man's attention from money to healing which was needed so much more, but was beyond the man's imagination, and commanded the man to walk.

Peter said, 'Silver or gold I do not have, but what I do have I give you. In the name of Jesus Christ of Nazareth, walk' (Act 3:6).

The command led to obedience and obedience to healing. Some things are more valuable than silver or gold, as Solomon found in relation to wisdom, and for this man's healing it, 'Is more profitable than silver and yields better returns than gold' (Proverbs 3:14).

Matthew Henry in his commentary on this verse in Acts 3:6 noted:

'This would enable him to work for his living so that he would not need to beg anymore; nay, he would have to give to those that needed, and it is more blessed to give than to receive. A miraculous cure would be a greater instance of God's favour, and would put a greater honour upon him than thousands of gold and silver could.'[146]

The healing was in the name of Jesus Christ of Nazareth, a term of reproach in the Gospels, but using it showed that it was actually a powerful name which could be used in healing (v6).

The man had faith in this name. The healing was not because the man was desperate for healing; not because of the faithful disciples; not because of the name and title used for Jesus, but because it was God's time for this miracle to take place as an act of his compassion and sovereignty. This was because there was a large audience ready to hear the Gospel preached which followed the miracle. God had chosen to do this and it only needed the mention of the name of Jesus of Nazareth to heal.

As the psalmist said, 'He sent out his word and healed them; he rescued them from the grave' (Psalms 107:20).

Peter helped him up (Act 3:7) to show faith and action at work, and as this happened the man's feet and ankles were first healed, and then his legs which had never before walked were so strong he jumped (v8).

He wasn't just healed and walking, he was healed and strongly exuberant in doing what came naturally to him in his personality.[147] As he realised he was healed his life was suddenly transformed and he praised and worshipped God who was the one who did the miracle.

Then, fulfilled the Scripture:

'Then will the lame leap like a deer—' (Isaiah 35:6a).

He had been enthusiastic in his begging and now he became enthusiastic in his praising. He had much to praise God for because now he had the means and opportunity to live a normal life at last.

He didn't get up shakily because he had no experience of strength in his legs; the healing was instantaneous and complete. It wasn't like improving from an illness it was a total and sudden healing. It was as dramatic as the widow of Nain's son who was raised from the dead, sat up and immediately held a conversation! (Luke 7:14)

The man didn't stumble. He didn't need assistance. He walked and jumped and many people around him recognised him as the severely disabled beggar (Acts 3:9–10) who always sat at the same spot by the Beautiful Gate.[148]

He had more than healing, he had joy! There is no wonder people took notice. It was a very public miracle and in a very public place and so there were many witnesses. This caused quite a stir and so he held on to Peter and John because he was so grateful to them for what had happened. A crowd draws a crowd and many people heard the noise and ran to see what was happening as the three of them moved on to Solomon's Colonnade. Recognising that the onlookers were amazed, Peter seized the opportunity to preach about Jesus (v12).

Signs of God's power were seen in this miracle; pointing to the truth about Jesus (John 3:2 and 14:11).

Peter preached and challenged his audience, 'Repent…and turn to God—' (Act 3:19) and to receive the Messiah for themselves.

This healing and preaching angered, 'The priests…the captain of the temple guard and the Sadducees—' (Act 4:1), who arrested Peter and John and put them in prison for the night, so, they couldn't do anything else that they, as the authorities, disapproved of (v3).[149]

Unfortunately for the officials, it could not be ignored and simply caused the number of believers to rise to more than 5000, not including women!

The effect on the large crowd is clear. There was no doubt about who the man was, or that it actually happened, as the miracle was in front of many witnesses (v9).

'They recognised him as the same man…and they were filled with wonder and amazement at what had happened to him' (v10).

The Pulpit Commentary speaks of Luke's use of these words, used only in his Gospel and here in Acts, 'Wonder and amazement…in other words, a very strong emotion of awe, admiration, or astonishment. It occurs elsewhere only in Luke 4:36, where it describes the awe and amazement which came upon those who witnessed the casting out of the unclean spirit from the man in the synagogue at Capernaum.'[150]

This was the outpouring of the Holy Spirit first seen in Acts 2:1–4, and the people were astonished (Act 3:11).

The healing could not be ignored, neither could the man who in full view of everyone, **'He went...walking and jumping and praising God'** (v8).

Final thoughts

[1] There is something very special about those with disabilities, and I believe Jesus on Earth had a special love for them and gave them lots of time. Consider for instance Jesus' healing of the man born blind (John 9:1–12), a paralysed man (Matthew 9:1–7), and Mary Magdalene who had mental health issues linked to demonic activity (Luke 8:2).

So, it is no wonder that disciples, given the power of the Holy Spirit after Pentecost, followed the example of Jesus by giving this disabled man in Act 3 all the time he needed.

[2] Jesus also gave a lot of time to individuals in one-to-one counselling such as with Nicodemus (John 3:1–15), the widow of Nain (Luke 7:11–17), and the woman at the well (John 4:4–30).

Similarly, we see Peter and John concentrating on one individual in this miracle of the man enabled by healing to walk (Acts 3:1–10). They had learned well from their Master and went forward in faith.

[3] The miracle prompted the sermon which was delivered fearlessly. Peter and John were very positive witnesses and preachers.

[4] The Early Church agreed and kept to their principles (Act 2:42), wonders and signs accompanied normal daily lives filled with the Holy Spirit, of which this disabled man's healing was a good example. Early Christians also followed formal Judaism as well as being open to God's prompting to go beyond the usual worship and practice.

[5] Peter and John saw rapid expansion of the number of Jerusalem believers but they also experienced opposition from the authorities and persecution from those who were religious.

[6] Matthew Henry (1662–1714), a nonconformist minister and author, wrote in his commentary in 1706 the following application of this miracle:

'If we would attempt to good purpose the healing of souls, we must go forth in the name and power of Jesus Christ, calling on helpless sinners to arise and walk in the way of holiness, by faith in him. How sweet the thought to our souls, that in respect to all the crippled faculties of our fallen nature, the name of Jesus Christ of Nazareth can make us whole! With what holy joy and rapture shall we tread the holy courts, when God the Spirit causes us to enter therein by his strength!'[151]

To be led by the Spirit is the right thing and limited or extensive miracles may occur, but those touched by God's Spirit in serving him will invariably be opposed by some.

However, 'Those who are led by the Spirit of God are the children of God' (Romans 8:14).

Questions to consider:

1. Is cheating at school, as I did in cross-country, ever justified?
2. Could we speak to a disabled person and trust God to heal them?
3. Does a miraculous cure indicate God's favour as Matthew Henry said about Act 3:16?

14 Paul and Silas

'Sirs, what must I do to be saved?' (Act 16:30b)
Full story: (Acts 16:16–40)

In my involvement with special needs, I encountered aspects of the prison service.

For two years, I ran the education block of a remand unit for 25 older teenagers awaiting trial, from the outer London boroughs. This was a modern building and had purpose-built accommodation and suitable resources. Sadly, but was burnt down by three young men on remand and was later demolished.

In one professional course, I undertook, I visited a very secure prison, near the city centre. It was built in 1825 and is now a grade-B prison. It was built to house 200 men but in 2013 had 408. It has always been overcrowded. It has a brick perimeter wall some 30 feet (9 m) high.

22 men and one woman were executed there until the abolition of executions in 1953. That was the year the only person to escape from the prison went over the wall. He fell badly into the Governor's garden and made his escape, but because of sustaining a serious leg injury was recaptured the following day and taken to the nearby hospital then re-imprisoned.[152]

Prisons, resembling what we see now, have been in existence since 860 AD when the first one in the UK was built by the Bishop of Winchester. One of the oldest in the country is The Clink (from which all prisons have acquired the nickname), dating from 1151, and was in use in Southwark, London to 1780. It is now a museum, and when I visited, it was the home of Britain's only full-time armour maker whom I saw at work.

The Clink and the secure prison I visited are grim inside and out.

In our next miracle, there is a very grim prison with conditions far worse than anything I have witnessed, but something amazing happened there.

Paul and his companion Silas[153] ministered together on Paul's second missionary journey (Acts 15–18), and went to the Roman city of Philippi (Act 16:12), founded in 356 BC in Macedonia, in what is now the North-East of Greece. Paul and Silas went regularly out of the city gate and down to the river to join those who met there to pray (v13). It was here that Lydia, a salesperson of purple cloth and a God-fearer, became a Christian (v14).

It was on one visit to the place of prayer that a slave girl with an evil spirit troubled Paul for days until Paul addressed the spirit to release the girl and come out of her (v18).

She was stating the truth about Paul but her speech was coming from the indwelling evil spirit, and so had to be dealt with. This greatly annoyed her owners who made quite an income from her ability to tell fortunes, and by predicting the future (v19).

The slave owners dragged Paul and Silas before the authorities, accused them of causing social unrest and complained that they were guilty of doing things Jews shouldn't do in a Roman colony. They failed to say Paul and Silas were also Romans. The magistrates ordered severe flogging with rods and they were thrown into prison with the jailer under strict orders to guard them well.

He put them into a doubly secure cell injured and bleeding, and their feet in the stocks (v24). Rev Beth Quick, an ordained elder of the United Methodist Church in South Carolina, gives an interesting insight into the conditions of prisons at this time:

'Prison was merely a holding place for those awaiting trial, and sometimes release, but often another punishment, or execution. Prisons were overcrowded. They were dark, and the inner cells, which Acts is careful to note to us is where Paul and Silas are held, would usually be entirely dark. Chains to bind prisoners were heavy, iron chains, which were particularly painful to bodies that had just been beaten and flogged.'

'Hygiene was pretty lacking. Food was minimal—most prisoners had to rely on visitors to sustain them with food and drink of any substance. Many prisoners would be kept together in one cell. It's a dreadful situation.'[154]

The accusers may well have been Romans and Gentiles and they cared little about faith, the slave girl, or about the prisoners being Jews or Romans. They only cared about their own financial loss (v19).

None of this deterred Paul and Silas who, despite their awful pain and prison conditions, were praying and praising God and were heard by the other prisoners who listened intently, and despite the time of day, they were worshipping God, 'Who gives songs in the night' (Job 35:10).

The Pulpit Commentary adds at this point:

'What a scene in the dark inner dungeon; the prisoners fast in the stocks, their backs still bleeding and smarting from the stripes, the companionship of criminals and outcasts of society, the midnight hour, and not groans, or curses, or complaints, but joyous trustful songs of praise ringing through the vault! Whilst their companions in the jail listened with astonishment to the heavenly sound in that place of shame and sorrow.'[155]

The Jamieson-Fausset-Brown Bible Commentary brings attention to the effect that the singing had on the other prisoners who were listening to them 'When the astounding events immediately to be related took place; not asleep, but wide awake and rapt (no doubt) in wonder at what they heard.'[156]

Suddenly, about midnight, there was a violent earthquake beneath the prison causing the doors to open and miraculously all the prisoners' chains to come loose (Act 16:26).

In other words, all the prisoners were freed—but none escaped. This whole event woke the sleeping jailer who felt a dereliction of duty and that he had failed in his responsibility to keep the prisoners secure. So, he decided to commit suicide because he was sure all the prisoners had escaped (v27).

He could see the doors were open but couldn't see any prisoners. Paul and Silas must, by their leadership, have taken command of the situation and stopped anyone escaping, and because of this, a man's life was saved in both respects: physically and spiritually. The prison was dank and dark, so the jailer asked his assistants for lights for the prison cells and realised at the same time his need for the light of salvation for his soul. He, therefore, ran trembling to Paul and Silas whom he must have suspected were wrongly imprisoned and had faith and trust in God.

He knew God had acted with power to protect them as God's servants, so he cried out the memorable words:

'Sirs, what must I do to be saved?' (v30b)[157]

Bible Study Tools staff in a blog bring attention to Paul and Silas triumphing despite unjust persecution, and this led to the jailer's conversion.

We read:

'Being persecuted unjustly for Christ leads Paul and Silas to joy rather than sorrow (Luke 6:22–23). Their praying and singing hymns prepare the other prisoners for conversion later that night.'

'The jailer's question, "What must I do to be saved?" implies he has already heard the prisoners proclaiming the way of salvation and their praying and singing. The miraculous earthquake and Paul's concern for the jailer's life strengthen his faith and lead to his conversion.'[158]

The sharing of the Gospel brought the jailer and his family to Christ and they were saved and publicly showed their new faith by being baptised. Even though it was the middle of the night, the jailer took the men to his home, cared for their injuries and gave them a meal.

Matthew Henry in his Bible commentary points out that a sincere work of God in the heart leads to a change of life brought in with a compassion which before didn't exist (Acts 16:33–34):

'The LORD so blessed the word, that the jailer was at once softened and humbled. He treated them with kindness and compassion, and professing faith in Christ was baptised in that name with his family.'[159]

The Holy Spirit brought him and his family into salvation (v34), and the actions of the changed jailer showed an immediate fruit of the Spirit (Galatians 5:22–23).

Amazingly, Paul and Silas remained for the rest of the night in prison until the magistrates ordered their release and sent their officers to arrange this early in the morning.

The officers did so and reported back to the magistrates that the two men were not only Jews they were also Roman citizens. This caused panic and alarm because the authorities had failed them as fellow Romans, with the status and privileges that brings. They were then respectfully escorted from the prison and asked to leave the city.

However, Paul and Silas went to Lydia's house and met her and fellow believers there, and enjoyed Christian fellowship (Act 16:15), 'Then, they left' (v40b).

Final thoughts

[1] Paul and Silas praised God even whilst in prison. Melinda Eye Cooper, writer for Crosswalk, a Christian resource group in Tennessee, tells us:

'Even though they had been beaten and thrown in prison with their feet shackled, they sang hymns and prayed. Their praise in such a bad situation caused those around them to take notice and listen to them.'

Luke records this clearly in Acts, 'The other prisoners were listening to them' (v25b).[160]

[2] Their praise not only helped them but also those who listened. God responded to their faith and worship by causing an earthquake which shook the prison, and the cell doors flew open. Not only that, 'Everyone's chains came loose' (v26b).

The psalmist said, 'I trusted in the LORD when I said, "I am greatly afflicted"' (Psalm 116:10).

[3] Roman law required jailers to take personal responsibility for prisoners. He and the authorities should have found out they were Romans and that they were being wrongly accused and imprisoned. The jailer woke from sleep and was about to kill himself, 'But Paul shouted, "Don't harm yourself! We are all here!"' (Act 16:28)

[4] Paul and Silas chose to stay in the difficult circumstances at the present time, when they could have easily escaped suffering the initial flogging and avoided the following imprisonment. By staying in their circumstances, they affected others for good. That example drew the attention of the jailer who realised there was something different about them and he wanted whatever they had.

Paul and Silas' example changed the jailer and his family's lives for all eternity. Melinda Eye Cooper adds, 'In an incredible act of discernment, Paul knew they must not run when the chains came loose, and the prison doors swung open. He knew God was working and using the bad situation for something good.'[161]

[5] The jailer and his family were saved because Paul and Silas stayed in the prison despite the fact they could have walked out through the open doors.

[6] The *Got Questions* podcast, supporting Christians from their base in Colorado Springs, shows how Paul and Silas learned to work together:

'From the biblical record of Paul and Silas, we learn the value of faithful companions and dedicated servants of the Lord in spreading the Gospel. Paul and Silas were like-minded and equally committed to the service of God. Whether they were praying for guidance in Asia, blazing new trails in Europe, preaching in synagogues, or singing in jail, Paul and Silas did it together.'[162]

Paul didn't plan to go to prison yet he was willing to submit to God, continuing to praise him even in shackles. His willingness to suffer and yet find joy in the middle of his challenges is something we all can apply to our lives.

'And we know that in all things God works for the good of those who love him, who have been called according to his purpose' (Romans 8:28).

Questions to consider:

1. Should Paul have healed the girl before checking with her minders how it would affect them, especially their income? (Act 16:19).
2. Were the jailer's family responding to God or to the jailer?
3. Paul and Silas were asked by the authorities to leave Philippi. Were they right to disobey? (Acts 16:40).

Final Days

15 The New Creation

'See, I will create new heavens and a new earth—' (Isaiah 65:17a)

Full story: (Isaiah 65:17, 2 Peter 3:13, 2 Corinthians 5:17, Revelation 21:1–4 and 22:1–5)

I spoke to a young serviceman recently who had been a Christian for about a year. As he took hold of the Bible for the first time in his new life he said:

'There was a joy and thrill which travelled through my body. I didn't have a clue where to start. I started in Matthew and thought I would get to know my Saviour first of all, then read through to John. Then, I thought I might as well learn about how creation was made so I went to the start of the Bible and started reading Genesis.'

'At first, it was a struggle reading the Bible, it was hard to focus and be disciplined in reading it every day, but eventually, as time went on and I was praying about it to the LORD; how to read his word and understand, the hunger followed suit and the discipline started to flow too.'[163]

Here was a new life in Christ: a new creation. Already, the serviceman was getting into a new book including the teaching of Jesus and the creation of the world. He was discovering how the book's author had brought him a new life.

The physical new creation

The new creation of the physical heaven and earth is because God said, **'See, I will create new heavens and a new earth—'** (Isaiah 65:17a), in which the creation *physically*, which was spoilt by sin and the Fall, is to be recreated; *spiritually* the new creation is the transformation a person goes through to be a citizen of the Kingdom of God by new birth.[164]

God promises through Isaiah that he will re-create the earth and gives good examples of the physical creation restored.[165]

The new physical creation will last and those who are part of it will have a name and identity which will never end:

"'As the new heavens and the new earth that I make will endure before me", declares the LORD.

"So, will your name and descendants endure"' (Isaiah 66:22).

Both physical and spiritual are important, but the Bible says much more about the second than the first, as this study will reveal.

The new creation of both the physical world and spiritual life is an amazing miracle and is the last in this book's selection of miracles. As far as the Bible indicates, the new creation of heaven and Earth will be the last of God's miracles. But just as wonderful is the re-creation of individual people who by faith through God's grace will populate this final sphere of existence.

The new completed and final creation will be the total establishment of the Kingdom of God and the re-born, re-created people are the inhabitants or citizens of this kingdom. They are children of the King and as such, princes and princesses. What an honour! What a privilege! What a royal position!

The first Bible miracle was the creation by God of the world and everything in it. The pinnacle of the creation was man and woman and they were created in the image of God and given free will. (This privilege was not afforded to the animal kingdom.)

The selfish use of free will by Adam and Eve led to sin and the Fall which has affected all people for all time and also affected the created world in ways we hardly realise. People and the world are no longer perfect. A close relationship between God and people was broken. We now experience and accept sickness, death and imperfection as being normal but one day everything not perfect will be renewed, restored and re-created.

As the Apostle Peter writes:

'But in keeping with his promise we are looking forward to a new heaven and a new earth, where righteousness dwells' (2 Peter 3:13).

Right-living or *righteousness* throughout the heavens and the earth will typify this new creation. This will be the *new order*. It will have replaced the *old order*. The transformation will be so much more splendid and glorious than anything we can picture.

John, the Apostle in writing Revelation gives us the fullest description the Bible offers in his penultimate chapter. He writes:

'Then I saw *a new heaven and a new earth*, for the first heaven and the first earth had passed away, and there was no longer any sea. I saw the holy city, the new Jerusalem, coming down out of heaven from God, prepared as a bride beautifully dressed for her husband.'

'And I heard a loud voice from the throne saying, "Look! God's dwelling place is now among the people, and he will dwell with them. They will be his people, and God himself will be with them and be their God. He will wipe every tear from their eyes. There will be no more death or mourning or crying or pain, for the *old order* of things has passed away"' (Revelation 21:1–4) (*emphasis mine*).

We then read of God's restoration work:

'Then, the angel showed me the river of the water of life, as clear as crystal, flowing from the throne of God and of the Lamb down the middle of the great street of the city. On each side of the river, stood the tree of life, bearing 12 crops of fruit, yielding its fruit every month. And the leaves of the tree are for the healing of the nations. No longer will there be any curse.'

'The throne of God and of the Lamb will be in the city, and his servants will serve him. They will see his face, and his name will be on their foreheads. There will be no more nights. They will not need the light of a lamp or the light of the sun, for the LORD God

will give them light. And they will reign forever and ever'
(Revelation 22:1–5).

(See also: Isaiah 65:17, Hosea 2:18–19, Matthew 19:28 and
Act 3:21).[166]

The spiritual new creation

However, as Wikipedia explains, 'The new creation is a
concept found in the New Testament, related to the new life and
new man (referring to the spiritual rebirth through Christ Jesus).'[167]

This transformation of individual people is made possible only
because of the birth, life, death and resurrection of Jesus, God's
Son, our Saviour. Heaven is a prepared place for prepared people
and the NT has much to say about how to receive eternal life and
one day live with God in heaven as individuals are gathered into a
worshipping community: the church. It is also called the Kingdom
of God.

Dave Bilbrough, singer, guitarist and songwriter released the
song, *I Am A New Creation*,[168] which echoes the words of Paul to
the Christians in Corinth.

'Therefore, if anyone is in Christ, the new creation has come:
the old has gone, the new is here!' (2 Corinthians 5:17), or 'If any
man, be in Christ, he is a new creature—' (KJV).

To be a new creation or a new creature, there must be a major
life change.

In terms of a transformed life, there are four examples which
show that the individual person must be shaped to fit the new life,
and not the life shaped to fit the person.

1. To look after and enjoy the garden that God had created,
    Adam needed a partner or *helper*. It was God's idea to
    create people: God the Father and God the Son together, as

the plural Hebrew word for us, translated into English indicates.[169] So, he created Eve as well as Adam.

'Then, God said, "Let us make mankind in our image, in our likeness…So, God created mankind in his own image, in the image of God he created them; male and female he created them"' (Genesis 1:26–27). For Adam, Eve was perfect.

2. When King Saul accepted David's offer to fight Goliath and he was preparing him as a teenager for this mismatched fight against the giant, he tried to get David to wear his own armour which must have been very large and heavy since Saul was a very big man.

3. David tried and failed to walk in it and so told King Saul that his best armour was his experience of trusting God; when his sheep were attacked by ferocious animals he killed them with just a stone and sling (1 Samuel 17:34–37, v45).

To Saul, wearing armour had seemed logical. The Philistines' best soldier was well-protected by impenetrable armour, so Saul thought David needed to be similarly attired.

David faced Goliath, 'In the name of the LORD Almighty—' (v45), his faith in God's protection was sufficient and perfect.

4. One of God's prophets was Jeremiah. One day he was sent by God to a potter's house to see what the potter was doing and there he heard God speaking. This visual- and audio-aid showed what God could do with people:

'This is the word that came to Jeremiah from the LORD: "Go down to the potter's house, and there I will give you my message". So, I went down to the potter's house, and I saw him working at the wheel. But the pot he was shaping from the clay was marred in his hands.'

'So, the potter formed it into another pot, shaping it as seemed best to him. Then the word of the LORD came to me. He said, "Can I not do with you, Israel, as this potter does?" declares the LORD. "Like clay in the hand of the potter, so are you in my hand, Israel"' (Jeremiah 18:1–6).

The new ceramic pot and the promised transformed people were perfect.

5. A fourth example of a transformation is when Jesus tells the parable of the Wedding Banquet:

'The servants went out into the streets and gathered all the people they could find, the bad as well as the good, and the wedding hall was filled with guests. But when the king came in to see the guests, he noticed a man there who was not wearing wedding clothes. He asked, "How did you get in here without wedding clothes, friend?" The man was speechless' (Matthew 22:10–12).

After the invited guests had made their feeble excuses for non-attendance, the king sent out his servants to invite the less fortunate people in society to his banquet and they were supplied with appropriate party clothes. The inference is that God requested his own chosen people, the Jews, to receive salvation but they refused and so the Gentiles were invited. These happily responded except for one who in his arrogance thought he could get away with his own terms and conditions of entry.

'Then the king told the attendants, "Tie him hand and foot and throw him outside, into the darkness, where there will be weeping and gnashing of teeth"' (v13).

His discourtesy to the host was met with exclusion from the event. The other guests were correctly dressed for the banquet and in appearance was perfect.

This brings into focus the spiritual implications of a transformed life, and what it means to be a new creation as a normal reaction to God calling people to himself, as Paul put it to the Christians at Corinth. This is what is meant by heaven being a prepared place for a prepared people.

Clarence L. Haynes Jr., author and contributing writer of Crosswalk blog, brings attention to the first word of 2 Corinthians 5:17. He writes:

'This is the first word we see in this verse. As a rule of thumb when you are studying Scripture, whenever you see the word therefore you should always ask what is it there for? Let us do that with this one. When you read the prior verse, you will get at least one indication of why this therefore is there.'[170]

What Paul is saying, as he explains in earlier verses (v14–16), is that when a person comes to Christ and accepts him as Saviour they are different and we should regard them differently, 'The new creation has come: the old has gone, the new is here!' (v17) This is what the Therefore is there for!

As Haynes goes on to say, there is a new beginning, a new relationship, a new identity, a new destiny, a new position, a new power and a new purpose. He expands these in a very helpful way.

Paul wrote to the Ephesian Christians:

'For we are God's handiwork, created in Christ Jesus to do good works, which God prepared in advance for us to do' (Ephesians 2:10).

We must not be afraid to be brand new with brand new values and a new Master whom we serve and get to know him and love him and enjoy the freedom he gives us.

The Got Questions podcast adds to this subject:

'To understand the new creation, first we must grasp that it is in fact a creation, something created by God. (John 1:13) tells us that this new birth was brought about by the will of God. We did not inherit the new nature from our parents or decide to re-create ourselves anew. Neither did God simply clean up our old nature; he created something entirely fresh and unique.'

'The new creation is completely new, brought about from nothing, just as the whole universe was created by God ex nihilo, from nothing. Only the Creator could accomplish such a feat.'[171]

Heather Riggleman, Christian social media consultant and writer from Nebraska, points out that the new life in Christ isn't for the individual to move straight into maturity as a Christian but that it takes time and effort:

'The moment we are born again we begin to grow like the seed in Jesus' parable (Mark 4: 26–29). Even as a new creation, we will still make mistakes. We will find ourselves saying things we shouldn't or doing things that don't align with God's expectations. But as we continue to keep our hearts and minds on Christ through reading and knowing his Word, the Holy Spirit gently convicts and lovingly corrects us.

'He shows us our sins and in turns because we love the LORD so much, we repent. We turn away from sin, ask for forgiveness, and do the best we can to live a life that reflects God.'[172]

N. T. Wright, a research professor at St Andrews University UK, rightly points out that, 'For the church's life and work in the present as well as the future, the church is to model the new creation in the power of the Spirit.'[173]

For the first time in history, Jews and Gentiles come together in oneness in Jesus, enabled by the Holy Spirit. This shows the world that the church is one in Jesus as LORD; the church is one but made up of individuals, and each one is a new creation.

Final Thoughts

[1] The *physical* creation will be restored so that there will be a new heaven and a new earth. There are hints at this in the OT, especially in the verses already identified in Isaiah. But a fuller

description of the transformation and its effect is found in the first four or five verses of Revelation 21 and 22. This will be an amazing miracle to see. It still lies in the future.

[2] The *spiritual* creation, the new birth, of those who come to Christ and find him as their Saviour is an amazing miracle which can happen right now. As we have discovered in 2 Corinthians 5:17, where it is expressed well, the old life has finished, and the new life has begun. It is not, however, a perfect and instantaneous work of God but more of a process as Christ becomes LORD of our lives, as our relationship with him grows.

[3] Jay Wilson, Pastor and Evangelist in Montana brings attention to the work of the Holy Spirit in the individual who is transformed from the old life to that of a new Christian.

He says:
'Life in Jesus is freedom from the old way of thinking. The Christian joyfully does what God wants in a concentrated effort to be like Christ. He believes that God is able to do exceedingly abundantly beyond what he asks or thinks, by the power of the Holy Spirit who works within.'[174]

[4] In an article based on interviews, Premier Christianity[175] reports that Tim Jupp, leader of the BCDO (Big Church Day Out),[176] where 40,000 attendees were expected in 2024 says:
'There is no greater miracle than someone meeting Jesus for the first time, and him changing their life.'

And Susie Aldridge, leader of DTI (Dreaming the Impossible),[177] another large annual Christian festival confirms as she looks ahead, 'We're expectant for miracles…the biggest miracle has got to be salvation. What else would you give your life to? It's amazing.'

The future event of the new heaven and new earth, and being a new creation and receiving new birth now are two aspects of a truly wonderful miracle. It was God's idea and he achieved it for his glory.

___

Questions to consider:

1. What does Peter mean by *a new heaven and a new earth*, in 2 Peter 3:13?
2. Who or what provides light in heaven? (Revelation 22:1–5)
3. What has God done in your background to equip you to be a Christian and serve others?

Concluding Thoughts:
Where Do We Go from Here?

One important job of a teacher is to challenge pupils. It's a way of getting them to think for themselves and really address problems rather than ignoring them or letting others solve them. I've found over the years you don't have to know the answers before you ask the questions.

Often it is best not to and that way you don't have all the right and perfect answers, but instead listen carefully to the pupils. I think Jesus caused people to think for themselves and try and discover their own answers as seen recorded by the Gospel writers:

Jesus asked the Pharisees, 'Why are you trying to trap me?' (Matthew 22:18b)

Jesus asked the teachers of the law, 'Why are you thinking these things?'

(Mark 2:8b)

Jesus asked the disciples, 'Why are you sleeping?' (Luke 22:46a)

Jesus asked Pilate, 'Is that your own idea…or did others talk to you about me?' (John 18:34)

We have therefore been asking questions of the Bible in relation to miracles such as: What happened? What did God do? What did people do? What do we learn?

In the Introduction to this study, we accepted that God could choose on occasions, to work differently from the original laws he established. And this, we see enacted in certain situations. In summary, the miracles covered were:

1. Creation: **'In the beginning God—'** (Genesis 1:1a). God made everything just by speaking (Psalm 33:9).
2. Noah: **'Noah found favour in the eyes of the LORD'** (Genesis 6:8). In his life and faith, Noah was *righteous* and *blameless* (Genesis 6:9,18 and 7:1).
3. Moses: **'God led the people—'** (Exodus 13:18a). Under God's leadership, Moses and the Israelites left Egypt and God opened up for them the Red Sea to cross.
4. Joshua: **'Do not say a word until the day I tell you to shout. Then, shout!'** (Joshua 6:10). Joshua listened to God and so the people listened to Joshua.
5. Gideon: **'Go in the strength you have—'** (Judges 6:14). God used Gideon's tough circumstances to get his attention.
6. David: **'The battle is the LORD's—'** (1 Samuel 17:47). David's protection was faith and his experience of God.
7. Elijah: **'My father! My father! The chariots and horsemen of Israel'** (2 Kings 2:12). Elijah was seen as a man of God.
8. Jonah: **'Salvation comes from the LORD'** (Jonah 2:9C). Jonah learned through his experience to trust and obey God.
9. Jesus and the widow of Nain's son: **'When the LORD saw her, his heart went out to her and he said, "Don't cry"'** (Luke 7:13). Jesus conducted a miracle out of compassion for a widow losing her only child.

10. Jesus and the woman at the well: **'Go, call your husband and come back'** (John 4:16). In challenging the woman to be honest, Jesus helped her find salvation.

11. Jesus and Palm Sunday: **'What are you doing, untying that colt?'** (Mark 11:5). The donkey owners knew the LORD and so freely released the donkey and colt for his use.

12. Jesus: the Crucifixion and the Resurrection: **'And when Jesus had cried out again in a loud voice, he gave up his spirit'** (Matthew 27:50). **'The angel said, "He is not here; he has risen, just as he said. Come and see the place where he lay"'** (Matthew 28:5–6). Death and the grave could not keep Jesus.

13. Peter and John: **'He went…walking and jumping, and praising God'** (Act 3:8). The Holy Spirit used the disciples in healing.

14. Paul and Silas: **'Sirs, what must I do to be saved?'** (Act 16:30b). Praise in prison leads to a jailer's conversion.

15. The New Creation: **'See, I will create new heavens and a new earth—'** (Isaiah 65:17a). The miracle of the physical re-creation of the Earth is still to be fulfilled. Spiritual re-creation of the new birth for individual people is a miracle already happening now.

So, where do we go from here?

In my selection of 15 miracles, I have attempted to see things from God's perspective and see the part played by certain key people at the time. I became very aware that God uses tough times, and often miracles, to get his people's attention, and I must ask myself the question, is he getting my attention today? God always sees more than we do, and again I ask myself, do I see as he sees?

I must also face the reality that, as Peter Kerridge, (d. 2024), former CEO of Premier Christian Trust reminded people, 'The

LORD of the universe is the father of miracles. He has a history of supernatural transformation.'[178]

He is LORD of the big things, such as the universe, and LORD of the comparatively little things such as the heart of an individual person committed to him.

I find that God confirms his wishes by speaking to a person's heart, so I ask myself the question, can I sense his presence with me now? Miracles involving chosen people show that God wants us to be faithful in private before we can be faithful in public. So, I search my mind to see if there are things in my life which need dealing with so that I might live more faithfully in relation to and for God.

God is patient with faith as it develops, which begs the question, do I experience him meeting me where I am with what I need? I desire God to be the LORD of my life. So, I consider, whether can I trust him with my life, my family, my finances, my decisions, my possessions and my future.

I trust that a high priority for us is to want to honour God by believing in him and believing in his power to perform miracles. But first, individuals must show repentance, or sorrow for sin towards God the Father. Also, accept his Son, the LORD Jesus Christ as Saviour and receive the Holy Spirit to become a new creation. As we grow to know Jesus, we will accept him as the LORD of our life and want to bring glory to him by our obedience to what he tells us to do.

This is the normal Christian life, about which numerous books have been written.[179] This is God's way to grant us eternal life by our faith through his grace.[180] This brings glory to God and inner satisfaction. As the Westminster Shorter Catechism of 1646 puts it, 'Man's chief end is to glorify God and enjoy him forever.'[181]

I, therefore, trust that as we have been thinking of miracles and trying to answer some of the questions about how, why, where and when in relation to each of them. We don't just pass over what we have read but bring the living LORD Jesus into our situations and allow the principles of the miracles to challenge us and change our thinking and so enable our lives to be changed to be more like Christ.

As I stated in the Introduction, *Therefore, we must investigate the Bible and God's ways of working with confidence and with an open mind.* Miracles, as I discovered with strange things in the Bible,[182] allow us individually to make up our own minds, but we do need to have an attitude of faith.

One day, when God has decided we have completed our living and learning on Earth as a child of his, we will be able to see our Lord face to face and ask him for the explanations of mysteries and miracles for which we have searched.

The God of the Bible must have the last word:

'Make every effort to live in peace with everyone and to be holy. Without holiness, no one will see the LORD' (Hebrews 12:14).

Questions to consider:

1. Why were the Pharisees always working hard to trap Jesus? (Matthew 22:19)
2. Which miracle do you find in the Bible the hardest to accept?
3. Which miracle in the Bible is (a) your favourite; and (b) the one that challenges you most?

Notes

Frontispiece

[i] The Gutenberg Bible is one of the earliest complete bibles and the earliest major book printed in Europe using mass-produced metal movable type. It is an edition of the Latin Vulgate containing the Hebrew Old Testament and the Greek New Testament printed by Johannes Gutenberg in Mainz, Germany. About 180 copies were produced and 49 now survive. en.m.wikipedia.org/Guttenberg Bible; August 2024.

Introduction

[2] This was a challenge laid before Job by God who said, 'What is the way to the abode of light? And where does darkness reside? Can you take them to their places? Do you know the paths to their dwellings?' (Job 38:19–20)

[3] Lexico; lexico.com; Oxford, 2022.

[4] The Editors of *Encyclopaedia Britannica*; britannica.com, 1768. Now published online with annual revisions. The edition used was 2023.

[5] John Murfitt *The Kingdom* 2022.

[6] John Murfitt *Two Destinies*, Zaccmedia, 2022.

[7] Pew Research Centre, *What do the world's religions say about miracles*, National Geographic Channel, 22 11 2017.

[8] C.S. Lewis *Miracles* (p216), HarperCollins 2002 (original: Geoffrey Bles, 1947).

[9] Jill Duff Lighting the beacons' (p24), SPCK 2023.

1 Creation

[10] The story of the Trapp family singers; Released in 1959 as a stage musical and as a film in 1965, 20thC Fox. The words are from the song: *Do-Re-Mi*.

[11] *Oxford Languages Dictionary*, Oxford University Press, 2021.

[12] Creation and stories such as a worldwide flood appear in the writings of other religions such as Islam, Judaism, Sikhism and Hinduism. (It is quite probable that they used Jewish literature, particularly the Old Testament as their main source.) en.m.wikipedia.org/Creation myth, March 2022.

[13] *The Holy Bible*, English Standard Version, Crossway, 2001, (revised 2007, 2011 and 2016).
[14] Using the title of a song by Moroder and Whitlock for the 1986 film: *Top Gun*. Performed by the American band, Berlin.

2 Noah

[15] Ken Ham, *Global warming—Normal in an abnormal world*; Answers in Genesis (p101 and 1:1) Publishers, 2018.
[16] Got Questions Ministries, GotQuestions.org; gotquestions.org/had-it-ever-rained-before-the-flood-in-Noah's-day? 04 01 2022.
[17] Hymnary.org.
[18] The story of Noah's Ark was also common knowledge at the time of Jesus as Peter and his hearers took it for granted as part of their Jewish history (Matthew 24:38–39 and 2 Peter 2:5).
[19] This date, based on genealogical study in connection with Bible references give the date of The Flood as being about 2304 BC. This is according to Dr John Osgood, Australian Medical Practitioner and Bible Researcher and Chronologist, Bible Creation.com, 1981.

3 Moses leaving Egypt and crossing the Red Sea

[20] Abraham was born c2150 BC.
[21] The Editors of Encyclopaedia Britannica, britannica.com, *Exodus* 1768, Published online with annual revisions. The edition used was 2023.
[22] 1300 BC-1201 BC. In this century, the Exodus took place, around 1280 BC.
[23] This is why the festival commemorating the escape from Egypt is known as Passover (Exodus 12:11).
[24] This is assessed at 2,400,000 people. Etrug.com, Summer 2021.
[25] bl.uk/learning/cult/inside/goldhaggadahstories/escapeegypt/escapeegypt.
[26] *The Exodus Route*, The Interactive Bible Website, bible.ca; (03–2020). Also: Steven Rudd *The Exodus Route Restored* Klarna, 2005.
[27] From the Red Sea, it would take a further 22 days to Mt Sinai, their initial goal to receive God's law before going onwards to the Promised Land.
[28] bl.uk/learning/cult/inside/goldhaggadahstories/escapeegypt/escapeegypt.
[29] biblestudytools.com, *Crossing the Red Sea—Bible Story Verses & Meaning*, Salem Web Network, 2022.
[30] Tissot adds to his painting:

'When Moses took the Israelites out of Egypt, he could have made it to Canaan in a little more than a week, even though he was shepherding over two million men, women and children. Of course, we know that was not the route taken. Instead, he took them on a route that began a 40-year journey.'
The Jewish Museum Collection, New York, fineartamerica.com.

[31] Nicholas Poussin, *The Crossing of the Red Sea*, en.wikipedia.org, 1634.

[32] Israelites were called Jews after the return from the Exile beginning to leave Babylon in 536 BC. The name Jews was derived from the tribe of Judah.

[33] There was an angel in this cloud (Exodus 14:19).

[34] Moses returns from the mountain to the Israelite encampment and speaks with God in his *Tent of Meeting* (or *Tabernacle*), located outside the camp.

4 Joshua, the Jordan and Jericho

[35] Excavations at Jericho of this period reveal that its fortifications featured a stone wall 11 feet high and 14 feet thick. At its top was a smooth stone slope, angling upward at 35 degrees for 35 feet, where it joined massive stone walls that towered even higher. It was virtually impregnable.

[36] What should we learn from the walls of Jericho falling down? GotQuestions.org/walls-of-Jericho, 04–01–2022.

[37] *Seven Powerful Lessons from the Fall of the Walls of Jericho*, biblestudytools.com/bible-study/topical-studies/powerful-lessons; the-fall-of-the-walls-of-jericho, 24–07–2021.

[38] The Battle of Jericho; en.wikipedia.org/wiki/Battle of Jericho, 18–03–2022.

[39] In ancient warfare of this period cities like Jericho were either taken by assault or surrounded and taken by siege and the people starved into submission. Its invaders might try to weaken the stone walls with fire or by tunnelling, or they might simply heap up a mountain of earth to serve as a ramp. Each of these methods of assault took weeks or months, and the attacking force usually suffered heavy losses.

However, in the book of Joshua, the strategy to conquer the city of Jericho in six days of preparation and one day's assault was intriguing in two ways. Firstly, it was devised by God himself, and secondly, humanly speaking, it was a foolish plan which would seriously unsettle the people of Jericho. A plan like this had never been encountered before. However, because God was behind it, that made it the right plan.

[40] The number seven in the Bible is very important. It often symbolises completion or perfection. Genesis tells us that God created the heavens and the Earth in six days, and upon completion, he rested on the seventh day (Genesis 1 and 2:1–2). This set the pattern for the future of God's people. At Jericho, there were seven days, seven priests, seven trumpets and seven marches around the city of the seventh day. (See: What Is the Biblical Significance of the Number 7? christianity.com, 31 01 2020).

[41] biblestudytools.com/bible-stories/battle-of-jericho, 07–08–2018.

[42] At the time the book of Joshua was being written, Rahab was still with the Israelites with whom she had settled (Joshua 6:25b).

[43] Jesus said, 'It is important to hear God and obey him' (Luke 11:28). For Joshua, this was a link between faith and works. In the NT, James speaks of this (James 2:26).

5 Gideon

[44] faithward.org.

[45] lifeway.com, 01–01–2014.

[46] *Gideon*, en.wikipedia.org, 09–02–2022.

[47] The Angel of the LORD, or *the LORD's angelic messenger* (Judges 6:11 NET) (NET is the New English Translation, Thomas Nelson 2001, online 10–09–2020).

[48] The OT principle is that if anyone sees God who is holy, they will die as a result. We read, "But", (*God said to Moses*), "you cannot see my face, for no one may see me and live"' (Exodus 33:20) (*Insertion mine*).

[49] whatchristianswanttoknow.com/gideon-bible-story-summary-with-lesson/#ixzz7ON9WLJ97.

[50] whatchristianswanttoknow.com, Ibid.

[51] C.S. Lewis; *The Problem of Pain* (p93), Collins, (original publisher Geoffrey Bles1940) 2015.

[52] We are not told that Gideon understood that the Israelite idolatry was the cause of the oppression by the Midianites (Judges 6:13). In being called to be the leader, Gideon argued that he didn't have the right background. He said he was the least in his family and his family were the weakest clan in his tribe of Manasseh.

He was unsure he could gain victory in war (v15) showing *his* doubts, but when he was convinced God was with him, he went forward in faith into battle (v22–24 and 7:1). The battle was about 1208 BC. About 1205 years later there was another person, this time a young woman from a poor background, who questioned *her* calling: that was Mary, soon to be the mother of Jesus.

Gabriel was sent by God to visit her with the news, 'Greetings, you who are highly favoured! The LORD is with you. Mary was greatly troubled—' (Luke 1:28–29a). This makes an interesting comparison!

[53] In terms of who is in ultimate charge of the people of Israel, under the Patriarch leaders of Abraham, Isaac, Jacob, Joseph and Moses, there was a *Theocracy*, with God as King. This developed into *Judges* and includes: Othniel, Ehud, Shamgar, Deborah, Gideon, Tola, Jair, Jephthah, Ibzan, Elon, Abdon and Samson (in the book: Judges), then Eli and lastly, Samuel (in 1 Samuel).

This led to the *Monarchy* where we meet Saul, David, Solomon and other kings who followed them in the divided kingdom with kings of the Northern Kingdom and Kings of the Southern Kingdom. Then came the Exile and upon the return of the captives there was just one kingdom. (en.wikipedia.org. *The Judges*). (See also, John Murfitt, *The Kingdom*, 2022).

6 David

[54] Arthur Arnott, *Only a Boy Called David*, The Hymn Society, 1931. Hymnary.org, gives the background. The song has been copied, adapted and issued many times since its first issue.

[55] As I write this the war between Russia and Ukraine is raging. It is interesting that the current richest man in the world (Elon Musk, b 1971, CEO of Tesla and Chief Engineer of SpaceX, worth £203 Bn), has offered to settle things by a one-to-one fight with the Russian president (Vladimir Putin, b 1952), and the prize is Ukraine without further bloodshed, but the offer wasn't accepted. I wonder if the two of them know of this similar offer in 1 Samuel 17?

[56] According to 1 Samuel 14:47–48, Saul fought against Moab, Ammon, Edom and the kings of Zobah with great success earlier in his reign.

[57] Scholars believe he may have descended from the Anakim, who were ancestors of a race of giants living in Canaan when Joshua and Caleb led the people of Israel into the Promised Land (Joshua 15:13–14).

[58] This last point is a critical one. David would not let God be mocked.

[59] There were obviously some family tensions as in Joseph's household before his brothers sold him to traders and he went to Egypt. Eliab, the oldest brother of David, suggests his youngest brother has just come to view the battle. He was presumably as embarrassed about the situation as the king was since he was also on the front line as an experienced soldier and yet silenced by fear and opposition.

[60] 2 Samuel 21:16–22, especially the last verse, explains that there were at least four other Philistine giants. One is specifically name as a brother of Goliath. Three more giants who were killed may also have been brothers of Goliath. biblestudy.org.

[61] Many times, when it was quiet and with little to do, I can imagine David practicing sling shots.

[62] Wikipedia.org. 26–03–2022.

[63] learnreligions.com; 2–05–2019.

[64] Bible Study Tools Staff, BibleStudyTools.com, 26–01–2022.

[65] Bible Study Tools Staff, Ibid.

[66] Bible Study Tools Staff, Ibid.

[67] whatchristianswanttoknow.com/5–everyday-life-lessons-learned-from-the-david-and-goliath-bible-story/#ixzz7Olbd2dn4.

7 Elijah

[68] David Sanford, Contributing Writer *Elijah*, Crosswalk.com; Christianity.com, 09–02–2021.

[69] Orthodox Jews celebrate the Passover (now called Passover sedar: home ritual), in a traditional way over the eight-day festival and they still provide a glass of wine, as a minimum, for Elijah; some Jewish families set a place for him. Time.com-passover-history-traditions, 02 03 2020.

[70] *Elijah*, en.wikipedia.org, 30–03–2022.

[71] For example, others speak of 900 BC-801 BC, *Elijah*, britannica.com.

[72] Robert I Bradshaw, *Elijah*, Biblical Studies.co.uk, 1999.

[73] New Bible Dictionary (p323), Tyndale, 1982.

[74] The Editors of Encyclopaedia Britannica, *Elijah*, britannica.com, 20–07–1998.

[75] En.wikipedia.org, *Elijah*.

[76] David Mandel, The Jewish Publication Society, myjewishlearning.com.

[77] Robert I Bradshaw, *Elijah*, Biblical Studies.co.uk, 1999.

[78] The Society for Old Testament Study, *Elijah*, sots.ac.uk.

[79] *Who was Elijah in the Bible?* gotquestions.org, 04–01–2022.

[80] W. Garrett Horder, Hymnary.org.

[81] *Dear LORD and Father of Mankind* was adapted from Quaker John Greenleaf Whittier's poem: *The Brewing of Soma* (1872) by Garrett Horder, Congregational Hymns, 1884.

[82] There were also a number of occasions when he verified the prophecy of Malachi as referring to the coming of John the Baptist in the likeness of Elijah. God says, 'See, I will send the Prophet Elijah to you before that great and dreadful day of the LORD comes' (Malachi 4:5). After Malachi, there was 400 years of silence from God and there were no prophets bringing messages from him until John the Baptist appeared.

[83] It is always very encouraging to see where the NT fulfils the truth concealed in the OT and the OT is fully revealed in the NT. It is here where Jesus affirms the OT and its characters and we see the application of OT faith and teaching.

8 Jonah

[84] metoffice.gov.uk › weather › case-studies › severe winters, the weather was believed to be the coldest since 1740. This 1963, winter was labelled *The Big Freeze*.

[85] Insight.org/bible/the-minor-prophets/jonah.

[86] biblestudytools.com/*Jonah*.

[87] Nineveh, founded by Nimrod (Genesis 10:11) at nearly 60 miles wide including all the adjoining cities, was the largest city in the world. It was destroyed in 612 BC by the amalgamation of five nations led forward by the Babylonians. Now, the Iraqi city of Mosul occupies half of the original site by the Tigris River.
Though Jonah gives the population as 120,000 (Jonah 4:11), these may have been just the children, the elderly and those with learning disabilities who *cannot tell their right hand from their left* (v11). Scholars have calculated a total population of more than half a million. This puts into perspective, the scale of the task allotted to Jonah who appears to be a lone evangelist.

[88] britannica.com-Jonah, 20–07–1998.

[89] The image of a large fish, called Leviathan, used elsewhere in the OT, is the embodiment of evil (Psalms 104:26) but created by God (Genesis 1:21).

[90] Ashurdan III (772–754 BC).

[91] en.wikipedia.org, *Jonah*.

[92] Matthew Henry, commentary on Jonah 1:17. (See my Textual Note 4)

9 Jesus and the widow of Nain's son

[93] Nain is a small village today (modern name Nein), located in the Jezreel plain, six miles Southwest of Nazareth in Galilee, two miles South of Mount Tabor. The name means *lovely*. It was quite a large town in the days of Jesus but is now mostly ruins except for the area of tombs on the East to where the funeral was presumably going. This is the only mention of Nain in the Bible.

[94] Only Luke records this miracle but he mentions the large number of people present who were witnesses to it. These include women, who would have greatly sympathised with the widow, and in whose minds this miracle was etched and who could have been the source for Luke's material.

[95] John Calvin, Commentary on Luke 7:11, *Calvin's Commentary on the Bible* (written 1536–1564), studylight.org/commentaries/cal/luke-7.

[96] At the larger funerals, some people were hired to cry. The procession probably consisted partly of hired mourners and musicians with flutes and cymbals, and partly of neighbours, friends and relatives. Jesus knew what time to set off from Capernaum to arrive at the town gate of Nain at the right time!

[97] *Death is not the End*—A Sermon on Luke 7:11–17, interruptingthesilence.com, 09–06–2013.

[98] (Luke 7:11–17), *Comfort in the Tragedies of Life*, redeeminggod.com. This story is very similar to the Widow at Zarephath, where Elijah trusted God for a miracle for her and her son to be kept fed and alive (1 Kings 17:7–16).

[99] Metropolitan Tabernacle Pulpit (Volume 34), 15–01–1888, Resource Library: Spurgeon Centre, Minnesota, spurgeon.org.

[100] In those days they didn't have coffins or caskets. They usually carried dead bodies in baskets and took them to a sarcophagus, which from the Latin means flesh-eater. There are still limestone sarcophagi in Israel. Once the body was gone, the bones would be buried. The Jewish law taught that touching the coffin or dead person made that person unclean. Spiritual leaders of the Jews were not even to go near a dead body (Leviticus 21:1–4, v11).
But Jesus came and touched the open coffin and at first causing himself to be defiled in the eyes of on-lookers until the boy came back to life, then he wasn't a dead body!

[101] Matthew Henry, commentary on Luke 7:15. (See my Textual Note 4)

[102] Matthew Poole's Commentary (1669–1676) on Luke 7:15, Hendrickson Publishers Inc, New edition 1980, biblehub.com.

[103] Rev. Dr Professor Sarah Henrich, Commentary on Luke 7:11–17, workingpreacher.org, 06–06–2010.

[104] Sarah Henrich, Ibid.

10 Jesus and the woman at the well

[105] An unspecified time later. In context, you would hear this term used in answer to when something will be done or when someone will arrive. kernowchocolate.co.uk/the-cornish-slang, 21–05–2018.

[106] Samaria is also called Sebaste. This is where the story of the woman at the well takes place located on a hill northwest of Nāblus in the West Bank territory under Israeli administration since 1967. This is according to The Cottage Girls Group, Christian Research, Tennessee. *The Powerful Story Of The Woman At The Well*, rosevinecottagegirls.com. 2021.

[107] en.wikipedia.org, 26–03–2022.

[108] The Samaritans were a mixed-race people, who had intermarried with the Assyrians centuries before. They were hated by the Jews because of this cultural mixing and because they had their own version of the Scriptures and their own temple on Mount Gerizim.

[109] This is what makes Luke's story of the Good Samaritan so exceptional because the Jews regarded Samaritans as outcasts and second-class people (Luke 10:25–37).

[110] Grandson of Abraham to whom the Samaritans looked as the founder of their race.

[111] The woman was looking to men to satisfy her needs, but Jesus diverted her attention to the satisfaction he could give in the 'Spring of water welling up to eternal life' (John 4:14b).

[112] christianity.com, 07–08–2020.

[113] nationalshrine.org, 16–04–2021.

[114] *The Woman at the Well*, learnreligions.com, 07–11–2020.

[115] Avery Rimmiler, *The woman at the well: It's significance and what we can learn*, justdisciple.com, 26–09–2021.

[116] Avery Rimmiler, Ibid.

11 Jesus and Palm Sunday

[117] *Palm Sunday*, en.m.wikipedia.org.

[118] Towards the end of his life, King David organised for his son Solomon to be king and replace another of his sons the self-appointed Adonijah who made himself king.

David commanded, 'Put Solomon my son on my own mule and take him down to Gihon. There shall Zadok the priest and Nathan the prophet anoint him king over Israel. Blow the trumpet and shout, "Long live King Solomon!"' (1 Kings 1:33–34). All David's sons normally rode on mules, but this was David's personal mule (2 Samuel 13:29).

[119] The hymn, written between 785 and 821 AD has three long verses or six shorter half-verses, and is an excellent summary of the Triumphal Entry. It was translated from French by Rev. J.M. Neale (1818–1866) in 1854.

[120] Similar words of rejoicing are found in the Psalms:
'LORD save us! LORD, grant us success! Blessed is he who comes in the name of the LORD' (Psalms 118:25–26).

[121] Obedience to God and the peace which follows are closely linked in the OT (Leviticus 26:3–6).

[122] crosswalk.com; christianity.com, 16–02–2022.

[123] It is beyond the scope of this book to explain further Mark's source material.

[124] Where the Bible speaks of *The LORD* in the OT, it generally means the LORD God, that is God the Father, and in the NT it means the LORD Jesus, God the Son.

[125] John Murfitt, *The Kingdom* (2022). Note also that palm branches were also a sign of God's blessing in the OT, and will still be used in future events and worship in heaven for the same reason: to indicate God's blessing (Revelation 7:9–10, v12).

12 Jesus: the Crucifixion and the Resurrection

[126] They were carrying unleavened bread because there was no time for yeast to work in the dough to rise.

[127] Christians everywhere celebrate this meal we call *Communion, the LORD's Supper, the Eucharist,* or *Breaking of Bread.* The bread represents his body, and the cup his blood.

[128] *What is the Easter story?* crosswalk.com, 02–03–2020.

[129] Crucifixion was not unique to Jesus but was a common Roman practice. Criminals, such as the thieves with Jesus on crosses alongside, and others were routinely crucified in the Roman world. Perhaps, the most striking thing about the method of his death was that it was so common. The difference for Jesus was that he was innocent and had committed no crime as the witnesses at his trials showed by their false testimonies.

[130] Some Bible versions translate this as *Calvary* (Latin) or *Golgotha* (Aramaic). It seems to have been a common place for these types of executions.

[131] Jesus speaks a total of seven recorded times from the cross. (Besides talking to the thief and promising him a place in his kingdom, he prays, and has a conversation with Mary his mother, and with John regarding their future. He shows his humanity by saying he is thirsty. He declared that the establishment of his kingdom and conquering of sin and death was finished, and commended his spirit into the hands of his Father).

[132] Hymnary.org.

[133] Rev. George Bennard, hymnologyarchive.com.

[134] Mrs Alexander wrote over 400 hymns, many for children.

[135] Christianity is the only religion with a living founder and Saviour and the only religion which has the means to totally forgive and forget sin, pardon the sinner, and grant eternal life.

[136] This comes to pass if individual people come by grace through faith in repentance towards God, enabled by the Holy Spirit to accept Jesus as Saviour (Ephesians 2:8–9).

[137] 'Yours is the kingdom and the power and the glory forever. Amen' (Matthew 6:13).

[138] *How long was Jesus on the cross?* biblestudytools.com, 14–04–2022.

13 Peter and John

[139] Makaton, or *key word signing*, is a simplified sign language and an easy form of signed communication, or sign-supported language. It uses signs and symbols, along with speech, to develop communication, language and literacy skills. More than 100,000 children and adults in the UK use Makaton, either as their main way of communicating or along with speech. It was developed by three teachers: Margaret, Katharine and Tony in 1983. This formed its name.

[140] Peter and John both had a brother in the 12 disciples of Jesus. Peter's brother was Andrew, and John's brother was James. This was seen in the sending out in twos when Jesus sent the 12 out as part of their witness and training. Peter and John had a very close bond after Jesus' resurrection (John 20:2). Peter was known for his outspokenness and sensitive feelings, and John for his love (see Psalms 55:17, and Daniel 6:10 showing OT teaching on daily living emphasising prayer).

[141] Pentecost is the festival when Christians celebrate the gift of the Holy Spirit. It is celebrated on Sunday, 50 days after Easter (the name comes from the Greek *pentekoste*, 50th). Pentecost is regarded as the birthday of the Christian church, according to bbc.co.uk/religions/holydays, 23–06–2009.

[142] CSB Study Bible is the Christian Standard Bible, Holman Publishers, 2010, 2016 and 2017.

[143] The three regular times of prayer became 9 am, 12 noon, and 3 pm for faithful Jews (see Psalms 55:17). John Wesley (1703–1791), an English clergyman, theologian, and evangelist, was a leader of a revival movement within the Church of England and the founder of Methodism. He comments on the time being, *The ninth hour.*
The Jews divided the time from sunrise to sunset into 12 hours; which were consequently of unequal length at different times of the year, as the days were longer or shorter, (en.wikipedia.org).

[144] John Gill; Exposition of the Bible; online: en.wikipedia.org. This is a very large Bible Commentary by a single person and took 17 years to produce in nine volumes in 1763. He was a sincere Calvinist and a Hebrew and Greek scholar. He was Minister of the New Park Street Chapel which later became the Metropolitan Tabernacle in London in which C. H. Spurgeon ministered 100 years later.

[145] Tony Merida, The Christ-Centred Exposition Commentary Series, Acts, B&H Publishing Group, 2017.

[146] Matthew Henry, commentary on Acts 3:6. (See my Textual Note 4)

[147] Luke as a doctor would notice these medical details of the healing.

[148] This is according to John Wesley's Explanatory Notes (1755 and 1765). Wesley was a Church of England vicar, and Christian theologian, and on this verse noted:

'This gate was added by Herod the Great, between the court of the Gentiles and that of Israel. It was 30 cubits high, and 15 broad, and made of Corinthian brass, more pompous in its workmanship and splendour than those that were covered with silver and gold.'

He was writing in his Bible Commentary in 1755, called Wesley's Explanatory Notes. studylight.org./commentaries.

[149] The story ends with threats from the authorities and a prayer meeting with real power and an outpouring of the Holy Spirit (Acts 4:23–31). The imprisonment simply caused Peter, John and the Early Church to be even more determined in their faith and we read, 'After they prayed, the place where they were meeting was shaken. And they were all filled with the Holy Spirit and spoke the word of God boldly' (Act 4:31).

[150] Rev. Joseph S. Exell and Henry Donald Maurice Spence-Jones, Editors; The Pulpit Commentary, published 1880–1919, Edition used: Hendrickson Publishers, 1985. Studylight.org; biblehub.com, 2014.

[151] Matthew Henry, commentary on Acts 3:10. (See my Textual Note 4)

14 Paul and Silas

[152] (name protected) en.wikipedia.org/HMprison/theclink.

[153] Silas, together with Judas, are called prophets who, 'Said much to encourage and strengthen the believers' in Antioch (Act 15:32b). Like Paul, he was a Roman citizen (Act 16:37).

[154] Sermon: Voices from Prison: Paul and Silas, bethquick.blogspot.com. 15–07–2018.

[155] Rev. Joseph S. Exell and Henry Donald Maurice Spence-Jones, Editors; The Pulpit Commentary, published 1880–1919, Edition used: Hendrickson Publishers 1985, Studylight.org; biblehub.com, 2014.

[156] Jamieson-Fausset-Brown Bible Commentary 1871, Edition used: Thomas Nelson 2017.

[157] In preparation for this humbling action and words on his part seeking salvation, the jailer must have heard Paul sharing the gospel in the grim and dark conditions and heard the praying, hymn-singing and worship of God. Paul quickly intervened and saved the jailer's life and explained salvation simply as believing in Jesus, for he and his family to be saved from sin and to receive eternal life.

[158] BibleStudyTools Staff, Paul and Silas in Prison—Bible Story, BibleStudyTools.com, 28–01–2022.

[159] Matthew Henry, commentary on Acts 16:33. (See my Textual Note 4)

[160] Melinda Eye Cooper, *Faithful Lessons we can learn from Paul and Silas in prison*, Crosswalk.com, 19–11–2021.

[161] Melinda Eye Cooper, Ibid.

[162] gotquestions.org, Podcast: *Paul and Silas*, 04–01–2022.

15 The New Creation

[163] The serviceman is a Royal Marine: a branch of the Royal Navy.

[164] John Murfitt, *The Kingdom* 2022.

[165] 'I will make rivers flow on barren heights, and springs within the valleys. I will turn the desert into pools of water, and the parched ground into springs. I will put in the desert the cedar and the acacia, the myrtle and the olive. I will set junipers in the wasteland, the fir and the cypress together, so that people may see and know, may consider and understand, that the hand of the LORD has done this, that the Holy One of Israel has created it' (Isaiah 41:18–20).

[166] This is a selection of verses from: Knowing Jesus, *15 Bible verses about The New Creation*. bible.knowing-jesus.com/topics/The-New-Creation.

[167] En.wikipedia.org/wiki/New_Creation_(theology). 21–04–2021.

[168] Dave Bilbrough; Album: All Hail the Lamb; Song: I am a New Creation, Thank you Music 1983.

[169] *Strong's Concordance with Hebrew and Greek Lexicons*, Jennings and Graham 1890, a Bible concordance, containing an index of every word in the King James Version (KJV). github.com/bibleforge.

[170] *7 benefits of being a new creation in Christ*. Crosswalk.com, 26–04–2021.

[171] gotquestions.org/new-creation.

[172] Heather Riggleman; contributing writer. christianity.com, 08–03–2021.

[173] Prof. N.T. Wright, Research Professor Emeritus of New Testament and Early Christianity at St Mary's College in the University of St Andrews and Senior Research Fellow at Wycliffe Hall, Oxford. ntwrightonline.org, 2018.

[174] *The New Creation*. newcreationstudies.org, 2006.

[175] premierchristianity.com. *Together Again* (p34–39) 05–2022.

[176] bigchurchdayout.com.

[177] dreaming the impossible.org.

[178] Peter Kerridge, wrote a commendation in *Lighting the Beacons* piii, Bishop Jill Duff, SPCK 2023.

Concluding thoughts: where do we go from here?

[179] An example is *The Normal Christian Life*, Watchman Nee (1903–1972) 1957 (but using his sermons from 1937), with revisions to 2018, Tyndale Press. He was a Chinese Christian teacher and church leader ministering in China for 30 years.

[180] God takes the initiative. We respond by him giving us the grace to do so.

[181] The Catechism was written in 1646 by a group of English and Scottish Puritan preachers, theologians and lay people to bring conformity between the Church of England and the Church of Scotland. They based much of their reasoning on words reputed to be written by King Solomon which form the final verses of Ecclesiastes:

'Now, all has been heard; here is the conclusion of the matter: fear God and keep his commandments, for this is the duty of all mankind. For God will bring every deed into judgment, including every hidden thing, whether it is good or evil' (Ecclesiastes 12:13–14).

[182] John Murfitt; *Really? A traveller's guide to strange things in the Bible*, 2023.